Praise for *Pre* … *s*

“I must have received fift … ay PreachersNSneakers first pos … ow me knew it would bring to light questions we’d been asking in private for a while. I believe the conversation it began is essential, and few at the time were willing to get it started. The book *PreachersNSneakers* is a reminder that it’s always easier to seem than it is to *be*. It’s not just dunking on people. At the core, Ben is keeping people accountable by asking questions that are easier to ignore than confront, and I’m here for all of it.”

—Abner Ramirez
Recording artist, JOHNNYSWIM

“*PreachersNSneakers* started the difficult conversations around generosity, indulgence, responsibility, and accountability, and it will impact the Christian church for generations to come. Ben Kirby’s book is forcing us to have a conversation about some of the aspects of the social media–driven Christian lifestyle that we are not as proud of, while creating a new narrative that is giving us the hope to create a future culture where we introduce accountability into our spending habits as Christians while understanding that the culture around us has changed. *PreachersNSneakers* is a book that will help reshape the church during this critical moment for the next generation.”

—Erica Greve
Founder and CEO of Unlikely Heroes

“The lifestyle described in this book was the house of cards I once lived in—and loved. Whatever your religious affiliation, this is a must-read. The author asks tough questions about those who behave more like greedy celebrities than God’s servants.”

—Costi W. Hinn
Pastor and author of
God, Greed, and the (Prosperity) Gospel

"My dude BK has written a book that will be sure to drive meaningful discussion about money and fame in the church today. This book is funny and is for everyone, not just church folk."

—Justin Holiday
NBA champion

"As a secular fashion and Sam Harris fan, I was excited to open a @PreachersNSneakers book that simultaneously showcased tons of cool sneakers *and* made fun of materialistic, hypocritical Christian leaders. Instead, what I got was an engaging, sincere, self-aware, non-preachy, down-to-earth but deep philosophical discussion about contemporary American Christianity that everyone, regardless of political affiliation, would benefit from knowing. Yuck."

—Ronny Chieng
Stand-up comic, actor, correspondent on *The Daily Show*

"I came for the jokes, but I was truly impressed with the depth of honest insight and challenging questions. Haters gon hate . . . but this book is fantastic!"

—Chris McClarney
Recording artist

"PreachersNSneakers has managed to do the nearly impossible: be funny *and* important. Normally one cancels out the other, but Ben, through his content online and in this book, continues to pull it off. I truly believe if there is one thing that can heal us individually and unite us corporately, it's making fun of celebrity pastors."

—Dustin Nickerson
Stand-up comic

Preachers
N Sneakers

Preachers N Sneakers

Authenticity in an Age of For-Profit Faith and (Wannabe) Celebrities

Ben Kirby

W Publishing Group

Published in Nashville, Tennessee, by W Publishing, an imprint of Thomas Nelson.

Author is represented by The Christopher Ferebee Agency, www.christopherferebee.com.

Thomas Nelson titles may be purchased in bulk for educational, business, fundraising, or sales promotional use. For information, please email SpecialMarkets@ThomasNelson.com.

Library of Congress Control Number: 2021902320

ISBN 978-0-7852-3883-6 (SC)
ISBN 978-0-7852-3890-4 (eBook)
ISBN 978-0-7852-3891-1 (audiobook)

Printed in the United States of America

21 22 23 24 25 LSC 10 9 8 7 6 5 4 3 2 1

To my wife, Stacy
I love you with the passion of a thousand
angry Christians bickering on Instagram

CONTENTS

FOREWORD

Hi. It's me, Joel McHale. You might remember me from such canceled TV shows as *The Soup*, *Community* (canceled twice!), *The Great Indoors*, *The Joel McHale Show with Joel McHale* (wait, this list is getting depressingly long). Okay, so if you'd like the rest, please email me (joelmchale@netscape.com) and I can send you the first terabyte drive of my canceled work. My apologies—this foreword has already gone off the rails, which, coincidentally, is the name of my new show, *Gone Off the Rails with Joel McHale*. It's about trains. And there I go again.

Ben is going to be mad that so much of this foreword has been taken up with me talking about myself and not talking about his great book you're about to read. (I mean, what do you expect, Ben? I live in Hollywood, where we add self-centeredness to our drinking water along with fluoride and antidepressants.) All right, here we go . . . the foreword . . .

Look, I'm not sure what I'm going to be able to write here that'll make you want to read this book even more. I mean, you already bought the book, right? It's not like you're at a bookstore right now (Barnes & Noble is not a bookstore anymore—it sells mostly Funko Pop!s and cool phone chargers), scrutinizing forewords as a test to see if you'll read the rest of a book written by a completely different person. And it's not as if Amazon displays the foreword as a sample of the writing. (Oh, it might? Well, then I hope this isn't the cause of lost sales!) Here's what I'll say: read the Jack Reacher thrillers. Those novels are tremendous. Once you've gotten through those, you should definitely read *PreachersNSneakers*.

When I was first introduced to the PreachersNSneakers Instagram account, I laughed for ten minutes (even more than I did while watching that video of the cat using a door knocker). The account was so funny and insightful. It reminded me of my early days on *The Soup* (see, it's always about me; I basically just said I was funny and insightful). Ben has made the spectacle of these mega-church preachers—who follow the teachings of Jesus, who said to give up your possessions—wearing $3,000 kicks . . . fun. Ben made it fun, and some of the most fun came from the online reactions of the preachers responding to the posts they were featured in. We got to read classic excuses like "They were given to me" and "I used my book sales money." I especially liked the book sales excuse. That's like Saint Francis of Assisi buying a yacht with the profits from all of his bird feeder statues.

This book goes deeper than just overpriced shoes and the holy men who collect them. Ben engages us in a big ol' thoughtful discussion of capitalism and its relationship with America's version of Christianity. It's great. Now I'm going to go check to see if the Nike SB Dunk Low x Ben & Jerry's Chunky Dunky shoes are back in stock yet.

As Ben, formerly known as Tyler the Anonymous, says, "The Lord works in mysterious colorways."

Thank God for Instagram!

—Joel McHale

Chapter One

THAT TIME I BLEW UP THE INTERNET

How Can a Simple Joke Start a Movement?

I never meant to blow up the internet. Seriously. The whole thing started out as a joke one Sunday morning in March 2019. I had slept through church after DJing until 2:00 a.m. the night before in Dallas's Deep Ellum entertainment district, a wannabe Bourbon Street that sure smells similar. I had a monthly gig at a bar there that consistently attracted about five people over four hours, but hey, it was a quick and easy $250.

I rolled out of bed just after ten in the morning, let the dogs out, poured a cup of coffee, and attempted to purge my deeply embedded Christian guilt by watching worship songs on YouTube. The song of choice this particular morning was "Resurrecting" by Elevation Worship out of Charlotte, North Carolina, and it had all the traits of an evangelical hit: hipster vocalists, fog machine haze, and an arena filled with euphoric worshipers lifting their hands in adoration of the feeling—I mean, er, Jesus.

I should've been listening to the lyrics, participating in the praise and whatnot, but all I could see was lead singer Mack Brock's Yeezy sneakers, worth nearly a grand. Without my full dose of caffeine, I grew irritated.

How could a dude leading a worship service at a church be so blatantly unaware of the optics that his shoes portrayed? And how could his boss, Steven Furtick, one of the most popular preachers in the game, be preaching in front of thousands of people each week in a new designer outfit that most of the congregation could never dream to afford? Something felt off either in me or in the video, and I couldn't determine why.

Reflexively, I picked up my phone and posted an Instagram story saying, "Hey, Elevation Worship, how much are you paying your musicians that they can afford $800 kicks? Let me get on the payroll!" Like I said, I wasn't trying to throw the Christian religion into crisis. It was just a poorly informed joke for my four hundred followers, delivered with a dose of cynical snark.

I wasn't trying to throw the Christian religion into crisis. It was just a poorly informed joke for my four hundred followers, delivered with a dose of cynical snark.

Shortly after my video went live, my hometown friend Seth Jones—an accomplished DJ and producer based in Los Angeles whom I have long admired for his musical talents and seemingly effortless good looks—texted me to say that I should start an account with just that kind of stuff: Christian leaders wearing luxury streetwear. Apparently, there was a whole culture of "hypepriests"[1] on both coasts that I had no idea existed. I dismissed him, but he persisted. He said this could be "the next viral thing" in Christendom. As an Enneagram Type 3—the image-conscious achiever, if you are unfamiliar—I naturally loved the feeling of making people laugh and the idea that I might be able to create something unique. I laughed, he laughed, we laughed. Neither of us had any idea how right he was.

Nine days later, after what must have been divine inspiration, I started the PreachersNSneakers account on Instagram, where I posted simple iPhone screenshots of pastors and worship leaders next to the hefty price tags/ street value of the shoes they were wearing. The name took all of thirty seconds to create. As I was contemplating the idea of starting this account, I wanted to see if there were any catchy names I could give it. I thought to myself, *What rhymes with pastors, deacons . . . preachers? Oh, sneakers! PreachersAndSneakers? PreachersInSneakers? PreachersNSneakers! Ha ha, yes!* The Instagram handle was available, and I immediately copied over the posts from my personal Instagram to this new social media creation.

Within a week, the account had caught the attention of some notable Christian media personalities who boosted the signal, which alerted mainstream outlets across America to my odd little thought experiment. Within four weeks, I had grown from zero to one hundred thousand *real* followers and was appearing in the freaking *New York Times* and *Wall Street Journal*, along with *Esquire*, BuzzFeed, Hypebeast, Fox News, and pretty much every other mainstream media outlet imaginable. The *TODAY* show even asked me to make an appearance to tell my story and "confront" some of the pastors I had featured. Ultimately, I declined, as I did not see how that could possibly benefit me and my family, given how uncertain and uncharted this territory was. I had no strategy, agenda, or desired end state for the account, and this wasn't supposed to become newsworthy, so the idea of going on one of the world's largest media platforms to explain myself didn't exactly reduce my therapy budget.

The world's most famous pastors and their followers messaged me to say that I was divisive, that I was being a gossip, and that I would ultimately have to account for the souls lost (to hell, apparently) due to my posts. Let that sink in for a minute. Christ followers felt so strongly about my pointing to the value of their favorite faith personalities' footwear that they questioned my salvation and prescribed eternal judgment for my actions. You could say I'd touched a nerve.

Maybe the reason I felt so irritated at Mack Brock that day was due to repressed anger or dysfunction about my own relationship with wealth. As C. S. Lewis wrote in his famous book *Mere Christianity*, "There is one vice of which no man in the world is free; which every one . . . loathes when he sees it in someone else. . . . And the more we have it ourselves, the more we dislike it in others."[2] In other words, our anger toward others is often just a reflection of the anger we feel toward ourselves.

Now, I know what you may be thinking. *Okay, bro. You should probably work on your greed, but you're a layman business guy. You're not getting rich off tithes and offerings. Should a minister sell the gospel for personal gain?* That's a totally fair point, and it's one I want to wrestle with in this book.

I believe the brief national furor created by PreachersNSneakers is telling us that we Christians need to have an honest and uncomfortable family meeting to ask the tough questions this debate has spawned:

- Is it okay to amass fame from a religion started by a humble, impoverished Rabbi?
- Is it morally problematic to generate opulent wealth from the preaching, singing, and selling of the Christian gospel?
- Do we really believe that divine blessings are typically monetary, or is that just wallpaper to make us feel better about the religious systems we've built?
- Does a church lose something when it looks more like a Dave & Buster's than a house of worship?
- Is there space in American Christianity for celebrities like Kanye West or Justin Bieber to exist without distorting the good news?

- Is social media helpful or just a breeding ground for envy and comparison?
- And what about this: Is it okay for someone like me to put a spotlight on faith leaders' actions or lifestyles and leverage callout culture to effect change?

These questions go well beyond a pastor's choice of footwear, and if the past year of my life is any indication, countless Christians and non-Christians alike believe it's time we address them. So this is not a book about a silly account that went viral one time. And it's not really about preachers wearing sneakers (although we'll discuss many of them). I'm writing about something even bigger—a conversation we've been avoiding for too long.

In twenty-first-century America, three forces have united to make living as a follower of Jesus more complicated and nuanced than at any other time in Christian history: capitalism, consumerism, and celebrity culture. We are plagued by the seductive traps of fame, comfort, and the love of wealth that most people across the world never have to worry about. These forces are raising questions that most Christian leaders, perhaps due to fear, are brave enough to ask only in private. It's time to drag these questions out of the shadows.

Today, every facet of our faith is intertwined with capitalism. For a religion (or relationship, depending on whom you talk to) based on following a selfless Rabbi, there is so much commerce, branding, and advertising that it's hard to distinguish churches from any other media or retail enterprise. Churches have developed colossal worship and teaching conferences, often charging hundreds or thousands of dollars per ticket; pastors are writing and distributing books on a global scale; and the untaxed eight- and nine-figure revenues of megachurches are starting to gain national attention.

In twenty-first-century America, three forces have united to make living as a follower of Jesus more complicated and nuanced than at any other time in Christian history: capitalism, consumerism, and celebrity culture.

Does Jesus care about the millions of dollars flowing through His churches? Does He care that increasing numbers of people in cities live in immense poverty while His buildings and leaders enjoy immeasurable splendor?

In her book *Buying God: Consumerism and Theology*, Eve Poole wrote, "Consumerism is a mode within capitalism that acts like an electric current within it. Consumerism switches capitalism on. If capitalism is the hardware, consumerism is the software that brings it to life."[3] As humans who believe in something greater coming in the afterlife, we can understand that our churches would be filled with people trying to satiate the thirst that cannot be quenched with anything of this earth. Christians are at war with wanting to serve God and to fulfill the desires of our sinful hearts. Thus comes our dysfunctional friend Consumerism with his promises of satisfaction, new identities, and fulfillment through retail therapy. Many Christian churches seem to have shifted to conform to this trend, elevating physical goods, fashion, and commerce despite Jesus' lack of desire for such things.

Finally, the modern church is no stranger to celebrity culture. With the notable conversions of Kanye West and Justin Bieber—the pinnacles of superstardom—the convergence of celebrities and Christian culture is now at the forefront of the news cycle. Along with mainstream celebs, there is a whole subculture of celebrities born out of the evangelical ecosystem. Worship leaders, pastors, and recording artists are all attracting millions of followers, sold-out arenas, and attention from the paparazzi. What are we to do with the attention drawn to these talented performers and creators whose profession is literally to draw attention to Jesus? How can followers of Jesus also be die-hard followers of anyone else? These are questions that every Christian, whether a pastor or not, should be able to answer.

This book marks the first time that I am giving details about conversations I've had with faith leaders and celebrities from around the world. Though I've tried to give you my honest opinions and takeaways, sometimes I've concluded that the best I can do is sit with you amid the tension and say, "I don't know the answer, but I believe we should keep asking."

Plenty of critics have accused me of doing this for the "likes and follows." Ironically, the most vitriolic contributors to my comment section have been professing Christians, a fact that itself raises a number of important questions.

I expect these iPhone warriors will attack this book, too, and I can already hear their criticism: "Oh, this dude is such a narcissistic, self-righteous hypocrite. He starts an account to shame pastors, and when it blows up, he writes a book to cash in under the guise of trying to create a dialogue. Pathetic." I couldn't convince them otherwise if I tried, but enduring their wrath will be worth it if this critical conversation continues.

After the account and the discussion went viral, I immediately committed to use this platform, in all its messiness, as a source for good. That's the commitment I'm making with this book as well. As you read this and process some of my questions herein, please keep an open mind and consider all sides. At a minimum, I hope this book will encourage you to stop and sit with the frictions you feel, to seek understanding, nurture

After the account and the discussion went viral, I immediately committed to use this platform, in all its messiness, as a source for good.

empathy, and develop grace toward those who may see, experience, and express faith differently than you.

If you scroll through the PreachersNSneakers comment section, you will witness bickering and name-calling, most of which are unhelpful. Often, though, a calm, quiet, empathetic person will join the conversation and change the tone. My hope is that we can become more like that person—willing to hear others out, regardless of how tempting it is to snap back with some snark (pot, meet kettle).

Because this is my aim, the pages that follow include a heavy helping of self-critique of my actions and commentary up to this point. I still am grappling with whether it's fair for me to criticize the lifestyles of others, most of whom I don't really know, period. But I have concluded that it is definitely unfair for me to do so without fully examining my own heart and lifestyle choices. That's why I decided to reveal my identity to the world, to no longer live behind that dumb "Tyler Jones" pseudonym. I want to meet you in the middle of this messy conversation exactly as I am so that we can help the church flourish in this perilous time. I didn't start the account to do that, but that's what I want now.

No matter why you picked up this book or what you're hoping to glean from it, I want you to know that God loves you just as much as He loves the born-again version of Kanye West and whoever is claiming to be Justin Bieber's pastor this week. No matter what you think or feel or believe, you're welcome.

If you're here because you're embarrassed by what the Christian church has become in America, welcome.

If you're here because your faith has been diluted by consumerism, welcome.

If you're here because you think followers of Jesus should probably emulate His life, including His lifestyle, welcome.

If you're here because you're a Christian and love fashion, welcome.

If you're here because you're an atheist and hate religion, welcome.

If you're here because you hate me for starting all of this to begin with, welcome.

Everyone has a seat at the PreachersNSneakers table because, as we all know, the Lord works in mysterious colorways.

Chapter Two

HARLEY MOMENTS

Is It Okay to Get Rich Off of God?

Ruston is a pit-stop town along Interstate 20 in northern Louisiana. It's so small that you'll miss it if you blink. There is one Starbucks, one movie theater, and a slew of fried-food joints that keep the hospital gainfully patronized. Ruston has so little going on that when the first local Waffle House opened, the ribbon-cutting ceremony made the front page of the *Ruston Daily Leader* newspaper. Ruston also holds the distinct honor of being the college home of both NFL legend Terry Bradshaw and NBA Hall of Famer Karl "the Mailman" Malone. The best thing about Ruston might be the town's sinfully tasty peaches, if that tells you how exciting it is.

I love Ruston because, well, it's my hometown. And because it's my hometown, I can speak honestly about its charm as well as its shortcomings. My critiques emerge out of my love. You see where I'm going with this?

Since Ruston is smack-dab in the middle of the Bible Belt, it's full of every subtle variation of stereotypical church. When I was growing up, each church had something of its own brand identity. The Methodist church was the megacool hangout church, complete with a volleyball court where overly competitive jocks would spike on one another and eventually fight with their shirts off. The church also had an actual arcade room, where I spent my junior high years grinding *Halo* 2 with my homies. (Clearly I used to crush it with the ladies.) The Baptist church was the more traditional experience, but the Baptists worked hard to compete with the Methodists in the youth department. They had a building for students, fitted with all the Ping-Pong tables and thrift-store couches a fourteen-year-old could dream of. I'm not sure where the used-couch obsession came from, but it hit youth rooms in the early 2000s hard.

Ruston's "Bible church" was the nondenominational option for people who didn't like stuffy, tired traditions but also didn't go crazy and lift their hands while they sang. We met in an old office building down the street from Wendy's. This was pre–ambient, cinematic backgrounds—or even PowerPoint, for that matter—so we used overhead projectors for worship, and some volunteer had to literally scoot the lyrics down as we were singing. A real vintage vibe. Our youth room wasn't hip enough to attract the youths by itself. Our strong suit was "solid biblical teaching." That was our church's brand. Our senior pastor, Charles, was a respected figure around Ruston—approachable, business savvy, wise. He wore a suit whenever he preached, without exception.

My dad is a family-practice doctor, so we lived a comfortable but modest lifestyle. He and my mom took seriously their responsibility to give generously to the church. They donated so much in tithes and offerings that our family was forced to sacrifice some vacations and name-brand cargo shorts that thirteen-year-old Benny desperately desired. They cared so deeply about the success of our church and the flourishing of our pastor that they were willing to forgo the creature comforts my dad had worked one-hundred-plus-hour weeks in med school to acquire. This way of being Christian was deeply ingrained in me from an early age. I learned that it was our responsibility—it was *my* responsibility—to financially support our church leaders as if we were donating directly to pave heaven's streets of gold.

For most of my life, I felt pretty good about our collective sacrifices. That is, until one summer night when my family was sitting at the dinner table, gorging on my mom's nightly meal—crafted in her trademark Cajun style with an extra helping of love and butter. Midway through our meal, the table started to shake and the silverware rattled. I gripped the corner of the table to steady it as an obnoxious rumble grew louder and louder. My mom and dad went to investigate, and I heard Mom shout, "Wow, Charles. That is a *hawg*!" The rest of our clan followed her out the door and stood silent and enamored in front of the diamond-like glimmer of the beast's royal-blue paint and the perfectly polished chrome covering the engine and exhaust pipes; it was a two-wheeled behemoth of power and splendor.

As Pastor Charles pointed out all the bells and whistles of his brand-new Harley-Davidson cruiser, I remember feeling impressed. But when he left, my adoration was replaced by confusion. I had assumed that my family was giving up *luxuries* so our church's leaders could afford *necessities*. But this motorcycle was worth more than one year of my parents' tithes. That was the first time I realized that there is a somewhat fuzzy line between a successful ministry and a booming business.

I had assumed that my family was giving up *luxuries* so our church's leaders could afford *necessities*.

"Harley moments" force us to ask difficult questions about the relationship between God and mammon, which I'm told is just a fancy word for money. Should a religious leader who lives off the donations of others drive a luxury vehicle or live in a luxury house or, I don't know, say, take "a lavish African safari vacation on the church's dime"?[1] These questions do not always have easy answers, and there's a whole lotta gray, but they are worth asking.

I'm not the only American Christian to have a Harley moment, and because you're reading this book, I bet you've got a story or two of your own to tell. Maybe you felt icky after learning that your pastor has been personally profiting off materials produced on church time. Or maybe you haven't felt comfortable since you saw the

Rolex flash from under the cuff of your favorite pastor's cuff-linked sleeve. Maybe your skin crawls when you flip past a religious television channel and witness pleas for cash coming from well-dressed preachers standing on gaudy golden sets.

Many of us have ignored the discomfort we feel, and some have grown bitter. An honest conversation about what it means to follow Jesus in an age of capitalism, consumerism, and (wannabe) celebrity culture is long overdue. First of all, if you don't resolve these tensions, you will lack the confidence you need to cultivate your faith journey. Countless former Christians have walked away from the faith because of the bad behavior of church leaders.

But perhaps more important, if we ignore these questions, we won't have an answer when skeptical, cynical, and non-Christian friends voice their concerns about the state of faith in twenty-first-century America. When people see these displays of Christianity on their television screens and social media feeds, they often assume that is what Christianity is all about, and it's difficult to convince them otherwise.

An honest conversation about what it means to follow Jesus in an age of capitalism, consumerism, and (wannabe) celebrity culture is long overdue.

Some of the people featured on PreachersNSneakers

(PnS), who were photographed wearing pricey clothing, have millions of followers across all social media platforms, which exponentially increases their reach around the world. Sure, we can rejoice that the message of Christ is getting out to so many who may have never heard it. But that doesn't mean we shouldn't investigate whether this message is being distorted by wealth, success, and prosperity. Ignorance isn't just bliss; often it's a cop-out. And it serves none of us well.

Social media has played a unique role in this reckoning. Before its emergence, our disparate Harley moments stayed locked in our mental lockboxes. We assumed we were probably the only ones who felt this way. But social media and the popularity of Android smartphones (LOL—I'm kidding) has awakened many of us to the expansive community of believers who are uncomfortable with the state of Christianity and the way our most visible leaders represent it. No matter what your Harley moment looks like, if you're anything like the tens of thousands of PreachersNSneakers followers, you're ready to face the discomfort of these questions head-on.

• • •

A small-town pastor purchasing a Harley cruiser isn't a capital offense. It is not worthy of the front page of the *New York Times*, and it doesn't rank in the top ten most troubling religious events in the world. Not even close.

In the wide world of Christendom, my former pastor's Harley is just a minor blip in terms of pastoral wealth.

After Harvest Bible Chapel's lead pastor, James MacDonald, was ousted from his Chicago megachurch due to questionable behavior and financial mismanagement, the church opted for a forensic accounting report of the church's finances. Conducted by the law firm of Wagenmaker & Oberly at the end of 2019, the report showed that MacDonald had been compensated more than $4 million between 2015 and 2019.[2] This compensation included "house security improvements, office remodeling, lavish gifts to HBC staff and donors, lavish travel with others, tickets to high-priced sporting events, Elgin studio space improvements, big-game hunting, [and] clothing for ministry media events."[3] Forget about the poorer neighborhoods in Chicago; Pastor MacDonald was earning more than 150 times the global median income. The circumstances are a far cry from Saint Francis preaching on wooden boxes in the village square and sleeping under the stars at night.

Or consider the polarizing megapastor Mark Driscoll. When leading a church in Seattle, Washington, Driscoll had to know that about twelve thousand of his city's residents didn't have a roof over their heads.[4] But in 2013, a Mars Hill executive pastor, through a memo, asked the elder board to approve a salary increase for Driscoll from $503,077 to $650,000, along with a $200,000 housing allowance.[5] Is that wild to you? It's wild to me. The next year, Driscoll resigned from his church amid accusations of plagiarism, financial mismanagement, and verbal abuse of staff members. The church-planting organization he founded, Acts 29, also gave him the boot.[6]

Both MacDonald and Driscoll have since relaunched their full-time ministries and are presumably receiving much support from their most loyal fans. Pastor Driscoll even offered to send signed copies of his sermon notes in exchange for submissions to his email list.[7]

At the end of 2019, Ron Carpenter from Redemption Church and John Gray from Relentless Church—both well-known pastors and PnS regulars—became embroiled in a very public, multimillion-dollar lawsuit between their two churches over the ownership of their church assets. Essentially, Ron Carpenter, founder of Redemption Church, transferred the church and buildings in South Carolina to Gray, who rebranded it as Relentless Church. Well, come to find out, there was a complex lease agreement and rich "retirement" clause for Carpenter, totaling $6.25 million paid to him over twenty-five years.[8] This hit the news when Carpenter accused Gray of not paying on the lease agreement, the retirement payouts due to Carpenter, and the lease on the Cadillac Escalade transferred over to Gray.[9] (Somebody call my homie Dave Ramsey.)

When these news stories hit, I'm sure many of the people who financially supported Harvest, Mars Hill, and Redemption churches had their own Harley moments.

And when stories such as these hit the newswires, they bring to light not only problems within individual churches but also bigger issues when it comes to who—or what—Christians are really worshiping. Are we worshiping the Creator or the campus? The Savior or the stage production?

These kinds of stories hit close to home for me, even as an adult. My wife works in full-time ministry at a megachurch in Dallas. For her tireless work, she makes a little more than what a worker at Chick-fil-A earns annually. Most ministers are like my wife. They are doing selfless and often thankless work, usually for "normal" if not meager compensation. And they wouldn't have it any other way. Their calling isn't dependent on cash. But far too often, those at the top of the faith-filled food chains are raking in the dough generated by an army of worker bees like my wife. Is this what it means to be a professional Christian now, or is there a better way?

Far too often, those at the top of the faith-filled food chains are raking in the dough generated by an army of worker bees.

• • •

Some might argue that religious leaders like those mentioned earlier are just taking advantage of a system susceptible to corruption. There is a pretty standard stream of how this all works:

- A church sets up in your town as a nonprofit.
- The church hires a pastor or two and either rents or buys a building.
- In order to pay those salaries and bills, pastors ask members and attendees to donate.
- Many churches believe in a "tithe," which is 10 percent of each member's gross income.
- The number of those who opt in to this program is relatively small and can't cover the growing bills. (The Pareto Principle also holds true in churches, where about 20 percent of members contribute about 80 percent of funds.)[10]
- The church designs a flashy giving campaign and encourages "sacrificial giving."
- This money is used for better buildings, better staging and equipment, enhanced programming for young people, and better salaries and benefits (usually disproportionately paid to those at the top).

As the system drives growth, the swelling church inevitably starts to look more like a business. The more people who join, the more tithes and offerings are collected. And this is where capitalism comes in. The staff, elders, and advisory boards ask what a CEO of a business this size would earn, and they often use that as a baseline, or at least a reference, for compensation. One justification for this is, "These guys could make five times what they make here in the private sector because of their leadership acumen and charisma; they're actually losing money by serving here!" It's a fairish point, but should money and equality to the marketplace be the driving factor for whether a Christian minister takes a job? Regardless, the idea of making the church more and more like a standard corporation gives me pause.

The idea of making the church more and more like a standard corporation gives me pause.

Going back to the tithe: this commonly accepted practice was established through Old Testament law in Leviticus 27:30–32 and carried over into the time when Jesus walked the earth. In Matthew 23, Jesus rebuked the spiritual teachers of the time and called them hypocrites for upholding the tithe requirements but not the other important aspects of God's law, like justice, mercy, and faithfulness, calling them hypocrites. Ouch.

Fast-forward to today, and we see the tithe still exists in some form in the majority of modern churches. A small group of Christians believe church work should be strictly part-time, and no one from the church should be paid, but the vast majority, at least of those I have talked to, think that compensating a full-time pastor is completely fair. The final comp number, though, is when things tend to get dicey.

In the 1960s, the Supreme Court heard a case in which the definition of *pornography* was being discussed in regard to a controversial film. Justice Potter Stewart responded with words that are now notorious:

> I shall not today attempt further to define the kinds of material I understand to be embraced within that shorthand description; and perhaps I could never succeed in intelligibly doing so. *But I know it when I see it* [my emphasis], and the motion picture involved in this case is not that.[11]

When I had my Harley moment, I didn't know what it was, but I knew it when I saw it. And a lot of Christians I know also feel queasy when they see a pastor step onstage wearing an outfit worth the equivalent of a mortgage payment. These onlookers don't know where the line should be drawn exactly, but they have a sense it has been crossed. If they are among the patrons, they often ask why they are sacrificing to support a ministry that is allowing big homie to live large.

A lot of Christians I know also feel queasy when they see a pastor step onstage wearing an outfit worth the equivalent of a mortgage payment.

Especially when the organization is rooted in a Book that prioritizes the poor and doesn't exactly praise rich folks.

I've grown up in the church, learning all the popular Bible stories, even reading the Bible from front to back a few times. As probably many of you have also experienced, I've found it easy to glaze over some of the lesser-discussed narratives that God intended to impart wisdom on His people. One of those narratives I recently read with a fresh pair of eyes is the story of Ananias and his wife, Sapphira, in the New Testament book of Acts. The story tells of how this couple sold a piece of land in order to give the proceeds to Jesus' ministry. They tried to be slick, though. They kept a portion of the proceeds for themselves and gave the rest to Jesus' apostles, saying that they had donated everything.

Now, the apostle Peter was hip to the scheme and confronted Ananias to his face:

> Ananias, how is it that Satan has so filled your heart that you have lied to the Holy Spirit and have kept for yourself some of the money you received for the land? Didn't it belong to you before it was sold? And after it was sold, wasn't the money at your disposal? What made you think of doing such a thing? You have not lied just to human beings but to God. (5:3–4)

And then the story says that Ananias fell flat on his lying face and went night night for all eternity (my words).

Cut to act 2: Sapphira showed up a few hours later, oblivious to her husband's fate. Peter quizzed her on the sale price of the land, and Sapphira confirmed how much they had sold the property for, just as her husband had. Wrong answer. She dropped dead too (vv. 7–10).

Bible scholars debate whether God actually whacked Ananias or whether Peter did the deed in God's name, but either way, the message of this story is clear: God DOES. NOT. PLAY. when it comes to greed and the motivations of our hearts. This is an important message for everyone who says they believe in Jesus, and that absolutely includes those who are called to be public leaders of that belief.

Discussion Questions

1. What Harley moments have you experienced?
2. What do you think are appropriate luxuries for faith leaders to spend their money on? What about for you to spend your money on?
3. How could you use your resources to further God's kingdom instead of furthering your own?

Chapter Three

KANYE, KIM, AND CARL

What Do We Do with Christian Celebrities?

As a teenager in the buckle of the Bible Belt, I spent a lot of time at church and churchy-type events. The most coveted gathering a small-town Christian kid like me could attend was one of the big annual youth conferences. Only the upper-echelon senior high students could go. At my church, you weren't allowed to go until you reached a certain age because, I assume, our youth pastor, John O., did not want to deal with the foolishness of fifty newly pubescent seventh graders hopped up on Warheads and Mr. Pibb in a small, confined charter bus. It's hard to blame him.

When I was finally old enough, I got my chance to attend several of these ultraexclusive youth conferences. Smaller ones would come to our town, but I had my eyes on the prize: the true Woodstock of Christianity was happening to the west in Dallas. For these, we would all board a bus and drive to a megachurch, trying desperately not to be the one to use the on-bus toilet or forever sealing our place as "that guy who couldn't hold it." I imagine a lot of us still have that same fear on airplanes today. Oh, just me? Cool cool cool.

During our time at these conferences, our sleeping arrangement would be to literally throw Walmart sleeping bags on a gym floor. At the time, though, this was a freaking blast: kicking it with all my homies, playing sardines and slapjack, and gossiping late into the night about who we liked and why we were never, ever going to ask them out. The conferences were hosted in massive arenas that felt like an alternate dimension for a small-town churchgoer who was used to a hundred stacking chairs on Sunday.

The worship leaders wore Ashton Kutcher–esque trucker hats and ripped the occasional guitar solo, making us feel like we were at one of those rock concerts we weren't allowed to go to. The thundering bass, considered borderline sinful at the time, catapulted our hands overhead, something I never would have done at home. The preachers peppered their sermons with hilarious anecdotes, the hippest turns of phrases, and emotional takeaways that eventually led to teary multitudes "accepting Christ" with every head bowed and every eye closed. These religious figures were our celebrities. Leading up to the conferences, we would read their books and listen to their albums. We all idolized them, even if just subconsciously.

Even though the preachers and worship leaders were there, they weren't *there* there. You could not touch them. Or talk to them. Or even get within spitting distance. They were shielded by security checkpoints, bodyguards, and the occasional entourage. This was the first time I became aware of "greenroom culture" and the divide separating the Christian *us* from the Christian *them*. While we were sleeping on sneaker-scuffed church gym floors, the "talent" was lounging in luxury hotels and being treated to expensive dinners.

This was the first time I became aware of "greenroom culture" and the divide separating the Christian *us* from the Christian *them*.

If any attendees found a way to approach one of these preachers in transit to thank them for their ministries or ask them a question or compliment their sermons, a handler would quickly whisk the preachers away. Gone. The only way you could guarantee a moment of time with one of your spiritual heroes was to buy a book, album, or merch item and stand in line to get it signed. If you were lucky, you'd get to squeeze in a question before you were lovingly moved along by a conference volunteer.

The wall dividing religious elites from their adoring masses is not a phenomenon that's present only in Christian conference culture. It is on display weekly at some of the biggest churches in the Western world. It's relatively common for pastors to have private entrances, reserved parking spaces, security details, a gaggle of assistants, or personal handlers. I've even heard of churches where a volunteer was designated solely for the purpose of carrying the pastor's Bible.

Taking a cue from the celebrity culture craze that grips American society at large, many churches now function similarly to the rest of the world. Like Hollywood—which the pietistic often criticize—these institutions and their leaders celebrate and reward the "blessings" of fame, popularity, and influence. Pastors function like performers or spokespeople for their churches' "brands." How does this impact a leader's ability to offer encouragement and hope to *all* who enter the church's doors? The answer is often unclear. Whether intentional or not, a chasm stretches between the well-known "talent" and the normal folks who are being asked to sacrificially fund the talents' lifestyles.

Whether intentional or not, a chasm stretches between the well-known "talent" and the normal folks who are being asked to sacrificially fund the talents' lifestyles.

Each year the Passion conference attracts tens of thousands of college-age people to see and hear the hippest worship bands, the dopest Christian rappers, and the slickest preachers in the game. Those who are willing to pay more than a hundred dollars per person to get in the door get to stand in a packed-out arena, such as Atlanta's Mercedes-Benz Stadium in 2020, and breathe the same air as former-NFL-quarterback-turned-preacher Tim Tebow and reality-TV-star-turned-preacher Sadie Robertson. The experience is admittedly impressive, complete with fireworks, Jumbotrons, smoke machines, laser lights, gospel chops, and a catwalk rivaling Justin Timberlake's recent tour setup. YouTube it—it's wild.

Passion is just one of many conferences that spends bank on technology, stage sets, VIP suites, best-selling authors/speakers, and chart-topping bands. There is something to be said for performing with excellence, no matter what you do, but isn't it reasonable to ask whether spending so much money on production is a necessary luxury for those who make a living off the Christian gospel?

Marshall McLuhan famously coined the phrase "The medium is the message."[1] The way churches and Christian leaders operate within this worship-industrial complex sends a message. From where I sit, it might be time to take a collective inventory of the system we've adopted to facilitate "worship experiences" and ask whether that system is accurately communicating what we are doing in the name of worship versus the name of entertainment and comfort. To be fair, many organizations and conferences do fund and catalyze meaningful work: Passion 2020 raised more than $1.2 million for Bible translation projects.[2] My friend and *Vampire Diaries* actor Nathaniel Buzolic also credits the Passion conference as the pivotal moment when he started following Jesus. Pretty hard to put a price on that.

Almost all of the super-fresh pastors featured in PreachersNSneakers posts have hosted their own conferences, and guess who flies in to speak? The exact same flossy pastors who have other conferences to promote, with a handful of substitutes. These conferences include VOUS Conference, Hillsong Conference, ZOE Conference, Transformation Conference, Ron Carpenter's 212 Conference, T. D. Jakes's International Leadership Summit . . . and the list goes on and on. Some conferences even offer VIP tickets—up to $1,000 a pop—where ticket holders are given priority reserved seats and an exclusive meet and greet with Christian celebrities almost as popular as Jesus.[3]

There are plenty of good reasons pastors or worship leaders could give for why they can't be accessible to everyone. Some would be stuck onstage for hours if they committed to shake every extended hand, answer every question, and take every selfie. Like, they still gotta eat, ya know? I can respect healthy boundaries and the desire to go home at a reasonable hour.

But even if we understand why the system works the way it does, we can still question whether that system is fundamentally broken in some way. While it's true that celebrity pastors may need boundaries and limited access in order to function, maybe we should take a hard look at a system that makes pastors into celebrities to begin with.

In the late twentieth century, many American churches consciously adopted an "attractional model" of operating, which imagined the church less as a committed and involved community of people and more as an event or experience to be attended and consumed. The goal was to do anything necessary to spread the Word and attract as many people to the church as possible. The logic was that the more people you can attract, the more converts you will inevitably produce. Conceptually, it's just like a basic sales or marketing funnel, where you get the volume at the top and hopefully make a "close" (or conversion) at the bottom. In time, churches realized that the world of entertainment publicity and marketing could teach them a thing or two.

While it's true that celebrity pastors may need boundaries and limited access in order to function, maybe we should take a hard look at a system that makes pastors into celebrities to begin with.

The bigger a church grew, the more successful it was considered to be. Christian conferences as well as Christian music festivals followed suit. They are often run by pastors and leaders steeped in the attractional model. So it's no wonder they rent the most famous speakers and performers to generate buzz and attendance for the hipster Christian conference du jour. This model has come to dominate much of American Christianity, but at what price?

• • •

Pastors aren't just pastors anymore. They are also motivational speakers, corporate coaches, and leadership consultants. If you like the sermon you heard on Sunday from T. D. Jakes, Joel Osteen, Ron Carpenter, or some other famous pastor, you can hire that same person for your event on Monday. For the right price, that is.

Pastors aren't just pastors anymore. They are also motivational speakers, corporate coaches, and leadership consultants.

In 2019, former Hillsong New York's pastor Carl Lentz was a keynote speaker at entrepreneurship mogul Joel Marion's 100 Million Mastermind Experience, which boasts speakers "who are the absolute best in the world at what they do, and have all generated $100M+ in revenue, spent $100M+ on ads, or been seen by 100M+ people through their platform."[4] This was well before Lentz was ousted from his position as senior pastor after revelations of multiple affairs and "general narcissistic behavior, manipulating, mistreating people" and "breaches of trust connected to lying, and constantly lying."[5] Before his downfall, Willow Creek megapastor Bill Hybels was known for leadership coaching to high-powered CEOs and NFL teams. Bethel Church's worship leader Sean Feucht even used his notoriety as a Christian celebrity to run for Congress in 2020. This doesn't mean that most pastors, or even all of those I mentioned earlier, became pastors to get rich or famous. There are much more efficient ways to secure the bag. But once they become notable pastors, some of them, or their publicity teams, certainly have a knack for selling their services.

When PreachersNSneakers was blowing up in the media, Carl Lentz texted to tell me a story. Right after the *New York Times* article about my account hit the press, he walked off a plane at LAX and was immediately stopped by a TMZ reporter, who asked about my account and the discussion about Mack Brock's footwear. He said that these were fair questions, but ultimately every adult has the right to spend their money the way they see fit.[6] Funny enough, all the members of Boyz II Men were also on the flight, but TMZ ran right past them to interview Carl about PnS and pastoral finances. Clearly, I was not alone in my fascination with this cultural discussion.

• • •

As Christian leaders achieve full-on celebrity status—whether intentional or not—what happens when some A-list celebs attempt to become Christian leaders themselves? As I've dialogued with people about this phenomenon and why elements of it trouble me, I often hear this justification: "If Christians can convert megafamous celebrities with massive platforms, we can use them to reach the masses with the good news." Notice the word *use*, because that's what often happens. Celebrities who become Christians are often commandeered and used as props in the quest for conversions or even just distribution. This practical objectification changes actual human beings into tools to be used for a "greater good." Reimagining fame as an asset for Christian ministry is a far cry from the movement's origins that often highlighted the poor, weak, lonely, marginalized, and overlooked instead of the wealthy, powerful, attractive, and popular.

Part of the draw to newly converted celebs may be due to some Christians' views of modern Western persecution. This is rooted in the idea that the world and its pop culture icons usually oppose or even reject the Christian faith out of hand. So those cultural icons becoming Christians subtly validates that the movement is cool enough, palatable enough, mainstream enough to compete in the broader marketplace of ideas.

Cultural icons becoming Christians subtly validates that the movement is cool enough, palatable enough, mainstream enough to compete in the broader marketplace of ideas.

Kanye West created a worldwide stir (one of many in his complicated career) when he decided to take a turn into gospel music and started touring his Sunday Service in random, remote locations with only word-of-mouth invites going out to close friends. At first, this exclusive experience resembled a mix between soulful gospel music and a *Wild Wild Country* cult vibe. Kanye did not originally connect it to any particular religious affiliation. These performances were just his next wave of creative pursuits akin to his earlier pre-conversion hit "Jesus Walks." But all of a sudden, Kanye's language and demeanor shifted. He started testifying about what Jesus had done for him and speaking about his conversion to Christianity.

Soon, megapastor Rich Wilkerson Jr. started preaching at Kanye's Sunday Service gathering. Other PnS alums like Carl Lentz and Chad Veach were also seen attending the services, vibing out. Then Kanye released a full album not so subtly titled *Jesus Is King*, which was filled with Christian references and themes. He even did an interview with Zane Lowe in which he stated that he had asked everyone working on the album not to have premarital sex.[7] He also asked his wife, Kim Kardashian West, to dress more modestly.[8] Then he popped up at Joel Osteen's Lakewood Church in Houston to preach.[9] Around this time, Kanye was also on *The Late Late Show* testifying about how he got a massive tax return just after he devoted his life to Christ and later announced that he would be performing with Joyous Joel Osteen at his Night of Hope event at Yankee Stadium.

Pictures of Kanye with various celebrity pastors started popping up on social media. The coverage reminded me of when Chance the Rapper declared that he was going on sabbatical to learn more about his Christian faith,[10] and Christians suddenly joined his fan club. Even though I'm a fan of Kanye and follow his career, the cynic in me struggles to see the fanfare as anything more than an advanced publicity tour with Jesus wallpaper. Kanye has unabashedly shown that he thrives off intense publicity. After all, you can make a lot of dough in America by appealing to the Christian masses, especially if you're a life-change celebrity story. Look at how much new exposure Kanye has gained from shifting his narrative to the relatively untapped market of faith-based, secular rap. Sure, Christian hip-hop icons like Lecrae and Andy Mineo have achieved popularity of their own, but by making such a public conversion, Kanye was able to mix both religious and mainstream markets together and ghost-ride the whip all the way to the bank.

No one can say for sure whether this was an elaborate ploy or if Jesus really wrecked the rapper's world. Either way, we should ask whether pushing a brand-new believer into the pulpit two seconds after his conversion is the wisest route. Maybe we should allow converts—celebrity or otherwise—to explore their faith more deeply before hailing them as role models for the next generation of religious young people.

Kanye isn't the only one who has made such a turn. Justin Bieber also had a public and seemingly night-and-day conversion to Christianity that redirected the course of his career. Like many PreachersNSneakers alums, the Biebs loves him some fancy sneaks. There are paparazzi pics of him online walking out of Barneys New York in LA with Pastor Rich Wilkerson Jr., and and back when Carl Lentz used to be on speaking terms with J Biebs, he texted me to say he'd just left Flight Club—one of the most famous sneaker consignment boutiques, known for its rare and expensive footwear—with Bieber, who offered to buy him anything he wanted in the store. Carl jokingly responded, "Nah, I don't want to end up on PreachersNSneakers."

Maybe we should allow converts—celebrity or otherwise—to explore their faith more deeply before hailing them as role models for the next generation of religious young people.

Justin Bieber was publicly in a bad place up until around 2014, when he and Lentz started interacting more consistently.[11] Carl baptized him in NBA veteran Tyson Chandler's bathtub,[12] and from then on, Bieber started radically changing his life. He canceled his worldwide tour midway through and married his girlfriend, Hailey Baldwin. The couple claimed to have stayed abstinent until marriage in accordance with traditional Christian beliefs.[13] Justin went from a tabloid's dream to a well-meaning Christian dude trying to get his life on the straight and narrow.

The same questions can be asked of Justin Bieber as they are of Kanye West. Celebrities have been known to regularly engage in publicity stunts to reach new markets, so it's difficult to discern the credibility of what you read in entertainment news.

Celebrities have been known to regularly engage in publicity stunts to reach new markets, so it's difficult to discern the credibility of what you read in entertainment news.

Let's assume that Bieber—and every other celebrity who decides to claim Christianity in some formal and public way—is sincere. There are still questions to be answered. Like, what do you do once your new celebrity religious icon behaves in a way that seems counter to how Christians are called to live? Or says something that many Christians find to be less than appropriate for the calling? In one sense, it's amazing that these celebs have become associated with Christianity, serving as representatives of the same faith you have, but on a global scale with incomprehensible, often uncontrollable influence.

In 2020, Bieber released his newest album's debut track, "Yummy." The not-so-subtle lyrics make it clear that this song is about Bieber having sex with a woman or women. The easy assumption is that the song is about his wife, Hailey. But who can say for sure? The female "stallion" that Bieber sings about making "my toes curl" is vague enough that it could be anyone.[14] And herein lies the problem, because lots and lots of Christians believe that sex before marriage is, biblically, something to avoid. And many more of them don't want their pop-obsessed teenagers listening to music about sex. If a preacher-turned-celebrity did such a thing, we could expect that people might call him to a higher standard. But do the same expectations apply to celebrity-turned-Jesus-reps?

I personally do not care what Justin Bieber sings about or who he thinks has "got that yummy, yum." But every Christian should care about how the message of Jesus and the calling of those who follow Him are portrayed. The church's current relationship to fame runs the risk of watering down the Christian gospel and our ability to influence others toward true life change.

• • •

A little review: There are professional Christians who become celebrities for being super-Christians. This gets messy because it fuses faith with fame. There are also celebrities who become super-Christians for being ultra-famous. This gets messy for the same reason.

We can reasonably presume that the Biebs and Kanye are never going to quit their gigs as international superstars to plant a church or do a three-year stint in the 10/40

Window, but only time will tell. Outspoken Christians like Carrie Underwood and Chris Pratt probably aren't going to be doing middle-of-the-night hospice visits. Maybe they already do—who knows? And Chip and Joanna Gaines aren't going to give up their Magnolia empire to run a soup kitchen. (Actually, I don't know about the last one—Chip and Jo may surprise us.)

But after the invention of preachers-turned-celebrities and celebrities-turned-preachers, it was only a matter of time until a third category arose. A category that, in some ways, is more powerful than the previous two: the preacher-turned-celebrity who pastors the celebrity-turned-preacher. Say that five times fast.

I have foreal lost count of how many pastors are currently credited as being "Justin Bieber's pastor." The number has to be nearing a dozen. There are many perks for all parties involved when someone is named the pastor of a mainstream celeb. The preacher gets to essentially borrow the celebrity's fame, and the celebrity gets a spiritual adviser on speed dial. Any problem you have, you get a straight shot to the highest-profile religious minds and communicators of our time. Fame is one of those social currencies that you quite literally can be afforded via proximity. Now you have outlets such as TMZ, *Vanity Fair*, and *GQ* writing stories with titles like "Hypepriests: The Grail-Wearing Pastors Who Dress Like Justin Bieber."[15] It's not inherently bad that these publications are now writing about super-fresh, celebrity-aligned pastors, but is this the new metric of success that the mainstream church is adopting?

The way forward is not immediately clear. We can't expect the Biebs to just walk into a random church and not cause a congregational stir. American culture has made it impossible for mainstream celebrities to operate as normal people. Some churches in high-profile cities even go to great lengths to create a comfortable space for notable celebs, which seems to be a genuine display of their level of care for these types of believers. We should celebrate any person's journey toward faith, but when religious leaders create a quasi-aristocratic class in full view of their congregants, is it worth questioning if the church has swung too far to the other side?

There is a recurring theme in modern Western Christianity that can often be found on conference tees and Instagram hashtags: "Let's make Jesus famous." In most other contexts and periods of history, this phrase wouldn't make sense. The idea that Christians want to spread the good news far and wide is a virtuous one. But the idea that *fame* is an innate moral good, and that Jesus wants us to get as much of it for Him as possible, is quite a shift from Jesus' life on earth.

The idea that *fame* is an innate moral good, and that Jesus wants us to get as much of it for Him as possible, is quite a shift from Jesus' life on earth.

If Jesus actually wants to be famous and wants us to make Him famous—all while we're trying to emulate His life—it's a short jump to say, "Maybe *I* should be famous." Because if you are famous, well, then you can leverage your fame to bring Jesus fame too. At the risk of stating the obvious, I should point out that knowing Jesus' name doesn't make anyone a Christian, and it doesn't automatically make the world a better place. Jesus can be famous, and nobody's life can be changed for the better. The gospel does not revolve around just Jesus' name but rather what He did for us and the call of all people to trust in Him.

There is a well-known story in the Bible about Jesus wandering in the wilderness and getting tempted by the Devil. Matthew 4 says,

> Again, the devil took him to a very high mountain and showed him all the kingdoms of the world and their splendor. And he said to him, "I will give you all these things if you will fall down and worship me." Then Jesus told him, "Go away, Satan! For it is written: Worship the Lord your God, and serve only him." (vv. 8–10 CSB)

Power, money, and fame were never an end goal for Jesus.

Maybe the idea of "making Jesus famous" is just a clever turn of phrase used to make a concise point: we want to reach the world for Christ. But that requires more clarity. We should at least consider whether fame is the end goal, and if it's not, shouldn't we move toward changing that narrative?

Jonathan Pokluda once said to me, "God can use kings, but He often uses peasants." The Bible is replete with stories about pitiful, insignificant, nothing people being used in ways that change lives for eternity. The poor and powerless are called "blessed" (Luke 6:20–21), and the rich and famous are often chastised (v. 24). Along the way, some of us started living this in reverse.

Discussion Questions

1. Who is a celebrity you idolize? (My idols are John Mayer and Will Smith; I would freak if I met either of them.) How would you feel if he or she became a celebrity Christian? Would you be overjoyed? Cynical? Concerned?
2. What do you think could be improved in how we treat celebrities who claim to be Christians?
3. What do you find problematic about celebrity Christians? If anything, how do we change?

Chapter Four

BAD AND BOUJEE? MORE LIKE GOD AND GUCCI!

Does God Bless with Bling?

Growing up, I never considered myself a Sara Blakely–style entrepreneur, but looking back, I now recall some of my overlooked business ventures. As a cash-strapped preteen looking to fund my Pokémon card addiction, I launched several sole proprietorships that mostly failed. I tried baling hay on a local horse farm, which was the closest thing to prison I had ever experienced and convinced me that hell is real. I tried power-washing homes but quickly realized that the boredom and sunburns weren't worth the cheese, nor did I feel confident enough to charge little old ladies for something I had no experience doing. I tried flipping thrift store items on eBay, which usually resulted in losing money. I wound up with a closet chock-full of useless Goodwill junk instead.

To be fair, my options were limited. The only other opportunities to earn money for a young kid in my town were to work either at the local peach orchard or at the squash farm down the road. I tried those options a couple of times, and let's just say God wasn't calling me to either of those career paths.

Later in life I would try BMX racing, skateboard photography, and working a Little League concession stand. I also played low-stakes poker in my friends' homes around town (this later got me fired from the concession stand after we decided to host a poker game in the owner's house while the family happened to be on vacation—whoops). I tried selling rap beats that I produced on GarageBand, working as a drummer for hire, serving as a spotter for an auctioneer, and even dabbling (quite unsuccessfully) in the multilevel marketing world. The good news about repeated failure is that it can quickly teach you a lot about what you aren't meant to do in life.

Back to junior high BennyBoy: one afternoon I again brainstormed ways to somehow make money *and* feel fulfilled. I wanted to capitalize on my passions and talent, but let's be real, I also wanted to make as much money as I could with as little effort as possible. The only thing that kept coming to my mind was candy. Now, it's important to note that until I became a Marine officer as an adult, I was, ahem, a husky kid. (Depending on when you're reading this, I might have since returned to that blessed state.) I loved greasy food and fried food and all things sweet. This was the Deep South, after all. Come to find out, a business model existed that paired my obsession with delicious treats and my aversion to hard labor: gumball machines. That's right. You know, those clunky, candy-apple red, coin-operated vending machines that were placed in every tire shop and DMV office throughout the twentieth century. Those were my ticket to financial freedom—or so I thought.

I saved up $300 to buy two gumball machines, one with strictly gumballs and the other a high-speed triple globe with options galore, including Chiclets, M&M's, and cashews for the health conscious. My dad was able to get my machines placed in his high–foot traffic medical clinic as the exclusive gumball supplier of the building. My mom would routinely make Sam's Club runs to restock my inventory. Once my machines were up and running, I was earning up to $500 a month in quarters. That's a mountain of holographic Pikachu and Charizard cards. And, yes, I do realize that this whole venture was steeped in privilege, but hey, those cards weren't gonna buy themselves.

Shortly after I launched my gumball business, a friend of the family, who was also a business owner, asked me how it was going. I shared that my revenue was growing with an increasing profit margin, and I explained how shocked I was that someone like me could make so much money from selling candy. He's a person I deeply respect, who also has an incredibly strong faith. He reminded me of the importance of tithing as a person of faith running a business. Not only because the Bible teaches that we should give generously, he said, but because tithing inevitably leads to multiplicative success in your business. While I don't remember the exact phrase, he encouraged me with something to the effect of, "If you're consistent with your tithe, the Lord will bless your pursuits."

While our family friend was clearly just trying to impart wisdom and advice to me, a young doofus, this was the first time I considered a transactional type of relationship with God. It's what Duke University religious historian Kate Bowler calls "boomerang [theology],"[1] the idea that every good thing will inevitably come back to you. As America's foremost authority on the prosperity gospel and the person who literally wrote the book on the subject, Bowler knows about how prevalent this kind of thinking is. She has noted that boomerang theologies are uniquely American and originated more than a century ago, in part because Americans were trying to understand the difference between the so-called haves and have-nots.

Until that conversation with my family friend, I had never thought of the idea that my obedience as a Christian could somehow lead to material gain. So I searched the Bible to see what it said. Sure enough, in the book of Malachi, chapter 3, God said,

> "Bring the whole tithe into the storehouse, that there may be food in my house. Test me in this . . . and see if I will not throw open the floodgates of heaven and pour out so much blessing that there will not be room enough to store it." (v. 10)

If you read this verse—and others like it—in isolation, disconnected from the context in which it was written, you could easily use it to prop up this idea of boomerang theology. If you're looking for a mechanism to exert more control over your financial future, it's a great verse to write on your bathroom mirror and recite each morning before breakfast: "Give to God, and God will give back to you."

Until that conversation with my family friend, I had never thought of the idea that my obedience as a Christian could somehow lead to material gain.

After my initial conversation with our business-owner friend, this idea stuck with me, and I've wrestled with it ever since. Does God actually "bless" people with income, like my $500 monthly vending-machine earnings, in exchange for obedience and tithing? And if so, would God also "bless" a megapastor with a mansion or Lamborghini as a reward for doing good? And if that's true, what is the difference between God and my gumball machines?

In his book *Learning to Speak God from Scratch*, Jonathan Merritt argued that the key to understanding this kind of thinking lies in the definition of the word *blessing*. In ancient times, the Hebrew word for "blessing" was *barak*, which literally means to kneel or to bend the knee, because a material blessing was "usually passed from a person of higher standing to a person of lower standing, and the blessed person would kneel to receive it."[2] According to Merritt, in the Hebrew Scriptures a blessing was understood as a sign of special favor that might include "everything from a spouse to pregnancy, affluence to a general sense of joy."[3] The constant theme for the Jewish people, however, was that blessings were aligned with humility. Hence, bowing the knee.

Fast-forward a few thousand or more years, and the sister idea of humility has all but vanished from conversations about blessings. Humility is now a tool for flexing on the gram and not-so-humble bragging about all the "favor" we are experiencing—whether it be courtside seats, a job promotion, or a dope vacation in the south of France. Do a quick search on social media for "#blessed." At the time of this writing, there were 128 million Instagram posts that appeared on the "Explore" page using that hashtag. Some people even say "hashtag blessed" out loud when talking about how good their lives are. While mainstream culture has overtaken the notion of blessing, this idea has bled into Christian thinking and communities. (It's not just secular musicians like Big Sean and Drake singing songs called "Blessings"; more overtly Christian-leaning hip-hop artists, like Lecrae and Chance the Rapper, have hits by the same name.)

To many pastors and believers, this line of what it looks like to be blessed is becoming increasingly blurry. On any given Sunday, you can hear all the Pentecostal poster boys—from Steven Furtick, who in 2013 said his humble dwelling purchased for $1.7 million was a "gift from God,"[4] to Mike Todd, who pulls up to church each week in a matte-black Tesla[5]—preaching sermons with messages like "No one can stop God from blessing you (except you)."[6]

To many pastors and believers, this line of what it looks like to be blessed is becoming increasingly blurry.

Throughout the week, pastors' digital brand managers post well-curated Instagram clips of them and their blue-check homies talking about "the blessings God has for you" and "being prepared for the blessings of God" and asking questions like "Are you ready to receive God's favor for your life?" (For many religious leaders, *favor* is a synonym for *blessing*.) Surprisingly, these religious leaders usually avoid actually defining what they think *blessing* means. But the context clues are clear.

I grew up thinking that God's blessing was that we are saved from eternal damnation in a fiery pit of death. But these leaders take it down a few notches and connect blessing to dream jobs, wedding anniversaries, expensive vacations, luxury vehicles, and of course, rare sneakers. To be fair, many preaching superstars wouldn't claim they believe in the prosperity gospel and may not even be familiar with the term *boomerang theologies*. But the way they use the word *blessed* is similar to televangelists and religious hucksters from decades ago. It's cooler, chicer, more stylish, and "relevant," so you'll be pardoned for not recognizing the similarities. But a closer look indicates it is nearly indistinguishable from the prosperity gospel of old.

• • •

The notion that God blesses us with money, experiences, and achievements correlating to our obedience now pervades our culture. But what does this mean for the majority of people who aren't receiving all these divine handouts? What about poor people and abused people and abandoned people and disabled people and the more than 650 million people who don't even have access to basic clean water?[7] If we consider the size and scope of the human race on earth, we realize that the popular definition of *blessing* comforts a tiny subset of God's megafavored while excluding the majority of others.

If we consider the size and scope of the human race on earth, we realize that the popular definition of *blessing* comforts a tiny subset of God's megafavored while excluding the majority of others.

The US Census Bureau reported that there are more than 7.6 billion people on the planet today.[8] Around one-sixth of the population lives off less than two dollars a day. Theologian Ron Sider's book *Rich Christians in an Age of Hunger* wrestles with the idea that well-meaning and wealthy Christians—people who belong to a faith historically characterized by caring for the poor and marginalized—exist while the rest of the world lacks basic needs. Sider wrote this:

> We cannot know the exact number of people lacking minimally adequate diets, clothing, and shelter. And this number varies depending on harvests, war, and natural disasters. . . . More than a billion desperate neighbors live in wrenching poverty—and another 1.2 billion struggle to make ends meet on $2 a day.[9]

And yet God wants to "bless" us with that promotion to senior account executive? Are the millions of people around the world—Christians, even—just not good enough, faithful enough, anointed enough to tap into this exclusive holy slot machine? The fact that billions of people suffer through daily poverty stands in such stark opposition to the idea that God is here to bless some of us with a job promotion or a Tesla Cybertruck.

Remember Kate Bowler, America's leading historian on the prosperity gospel? After traveling the country for years, observing the messages these prosperity ministers were spreading, she had subtly begun to believe the popular notion of divine blessing. But then, in her midthirties when she was in the prime of her career and life, Bowler was diagnosed with stage 4 colon cancer. That's right, the person who sat with and studied the primo faith healers and your-best-life-nowers was battling an incurable disease that threatened her existence. While most of us won't face the horror into which Bowler was thrust against her will, many of us will have a life experience that calls into question our deeply rooted assumptions about God and divine blessings.

My friend Rachel miscarried her baby halfway through her pregnancy. The loss was followed by painful surgeries and unbearable sorrow. She's been as obedient as she knows how to be, so where is her blessing? Juli Wilson has to live through the grief of her husband, Jarrid, suddenly dying by suicide, leaving her to raise two young sons all alone. Juli loves God, so where is her extra scoop of divine favor? How are people like Rachel or Juli—or you—supposed to interpret these words from Steven Furtick's May 2020 sermon titled "Trapped in Transition":

> [God] isn't waiting for you to arrive before He blesses you. Regardless of where you are in life, God is already there. For everybody who is in transition: God is going to bless you on the way. You don't have to wait until you've arrived and have it all together; He can bless you right where you are.[10]

Or what about when Pastor Victoria Osteen said in a recent tweet, "When we live a life of giving, not only are we blessing others, but we are setting up blessings in our own lives. When you give, it will always come back to you."[11] Of course, you won't be able to find the post now because it was deleted/replaced after I retweeted it.

Those of us who claim to be Christians have to wrestle with this. Maybe you believe that God does, in fact, bless His compliant kids with loving boyfriends and Louis Vuitton duffels. But it must also follow that God is disproportionately blessing rich folks and white folks and Western folks. If you *don't* believe this is how it works, you must now search for a bigger, better concept of favor and blessings that offers space to all who seek God.

• • •

If only God had sent a representative to earth to model how we should view health, wealth, possessions, power, fame, and status. Oh, wait.

Jesus amplified the idea that the poor, weary, and beaten down are actually blessed, loved, and even elevated in the eyes of God. This seemingly proved that He was God's Son and not some poser with slick words, because that idea was so countercultural for the time—and it still is. Jesus could have been wealthy or charismatic, but instead He came as a baby in a barn and used a feed trough for a bed. Matthew 25 describes God at the end of the world saying,

> "Come, you who are blessed by my Father. . . . For I was hungry and you gave me something to eat, I was

> thirsty and you gave me something to drink, I was a stranger and you invited me in, I needed clothes and you clothed me, I was sick and you looked after me, I was in prison and you came to visit me." (vv. 34–36)

This chapter also provides us with God's words that "whatever you did for one of the least of these . . . you did for me" (v. 40). This is a shocking statement for those of us in the West who seem to have more relative wealth than we know what to do with. Jesus was seen as a Dennis Rodman–level radical for spending His time on earth admonishing the haves and blessing the have-nots.

Jesus amplified the idea that the poor, weary, and beaten down are actually blessed, loved, and even elevated in the eyes of God.

If Jesus sees the poor as blessed, then what does that mean for those of us who are currently #blessed? If we believe the Bible to be the actual words of God, then what do we do with this disparity? How can we exist in a world where billions are hungry, while we're tweeting that we're #blessed from our table at Nobu?

While Jesus' definition of *blessed* was revolutionary, the seeds of this idea were sown in the Hebrew Bible. There is a famous account in the Bible about a successful man named Job who was living the biblical version of the American dream: wife, kids, health, tons of real estate, livestock, and so forth. God saw Job as honorable and decent and was so confident in him that He allowed the Devil to impose undeserved pain and suffering on Job. This included losing all of his possessions and his children, as well as contracting disgusting diseases. God allowed this to happen to show that even in the midst of agony and anguish, Job would still see God as good and in control.

In the end, God restored Job to an even better situation than before, but this was only after Job had shown that his attitude was pure toward God regardless of circumstances. This wasn't like the end of the movie *Ocean's Thirteen*, where the casino critic won a huge jackpot after being tormented by Danny Ocean and crew. No, this was not compensation, because Job's suffering was not a punishment. God restoring Job's material wealth and family was never guaranteed. God would still have been perfectly good had He let Job stay in his downtrodden circumstances. God clearly had the power to give and take away the worldly things but cared so much more about the righteousness and attitude of those who say they love Him. While God eventually restored Job to a more livable standing, this story still provides a stunning indictment on the notion that blessings and curses equate to your individual level of favor with God.

Bottom line: God *can* use $900 Balenciaga sneakers or courtside Lakers tickets to bless someone—He controls everything—but this isn't the way He usually seems to work. According to the book of John, Jesus promised something quite different: "I have told you these things, so that in me you may have peace. In this world you will have trouble. But take heart! I have overcome the world" (16:33).

If any of us do receive even the smallest amount of success, notoriety, or wealth, we should adamantly be on our knees, thanking God for showing us grace and mercy with things that we absolutely do not deserve. There is no arguing that people have experienced financial and worldly blessing. At the same time, we shouldn't be following God in order to receive the world's equivalent of cheap carnival prizes. We should expect infinitely larger, more unimaginable things to happen. The God of the universe is the only One in control, the only One who can change someone's life, reverse starvation and drought, and perform literal miracles with no limit to their size and scope. God's love and grace, joy and peace, intersecting our lives in small ways—that's the blessing. Allowing us to have a relationship and an eternity with Him—that's the blessing. May we all pray huge prayers and ask God for everyday miracles instead of tangible trinkets that will inevitably lead us into ever greater discontent.

Discussion Questions

1. In what ways do you feel blessed?
2. If you're faithfully giving to your church, is it in the back of your mind that God's going to bless you? Or that He's not blessing you because your giving is below 10 percent?
3. What are ways you can bless someone this week?

Chapter Five

A NOTE ABOUT $1,000 SNEAKERS

How Can a Pair of Kicks Be Worth So Much?

There is probably a whole list of reasons why you may be reading this book. You may love the church or hate it, love the featured pastors or think they're wrongfully profiting off of tithes. You may have picked up this book because you love anything to do with the sneaker game, or you may just be here because you want to see what all the fuss is about and know nothing of these pricey kicks. This chapter is mainly for the last group.

The only reason I know anything about sneakers or streetwear is because of my friends Justin and Shekinah Holiday. I have known both of them since we were in elementary school back in North Louisiana, where I used to cross Justin over and hit my step-back three right in his face when we played basketball. At least, that's how I choose to remember it. Shekinah and I also ran in the same circles at church and attended the same used-couch youth groups. We even participated in a six o'clock Friday morning Bible study that we stuck with throughout high school (shout-out to John O'Leary and the Fab Five).

Fast-forward a few years: Justin and Shekinah eventually got married. Between Justin and me, one of us became

The only reason I know anything about sneakers or streetwear is because of my friends Justin and Shekinah Holiday.

an NBA champion, and the other is running an anonymous Instagram account from his home in North Dallas. I'll let you figure out who's who. Anyway, back in 2015 and about fifty pounds ago, I was on a Special Purpose Marine Air-Ground Task Force, Crisis Response (SPMAGTF-CR) deployment to Romania with Marine Wing Support Squadron 272 (MWSS-272) out of Marine Corps Air Station New River (MCAS New River) in North Carolina; the Marine Corps loves them some confusing acronyms. I was a young Marine logistics officer ('rah) tasked with leading a bunch of Marines and Sailors to support some grunts (infantry dudes) in Constanta, Romania. This was my first deployment, as well as my first time as the head guy, so I quite literally had no idea what I was doing (some things never change).

Before the deployment, I married my angel-woman of a wife, Stacy. Six months after we said, "I do," I was on a plane to a remote part of eastern Europe, leaving my new wife behind, both of us feeling a great deal of despair at the thought of being separated for seven and a half months. (This will make sense soon; just stick with me here.) While I was on deployment, trying to keep my Marines from breaking things and ending up in a

Romanian prison, Justin was picked up by the Golden State Warriors for the 2014–15 season as a backup shooting guard. This was after a long stint playing pro ball in Europe for essentially pennies. With his new NBA contract, he also got a product-only endorsement deal with Nike, along with a bunch of credit that he could use at the Nike players-only online store.

While many players get cash plus apparel deals, Justin was happy just to be able to get a few pairs of Nike PG 2s while playing with the likes of Steph Curry and Draymond Green. Up to this point, I didn't know or care about sneakers at all; I preferred to wear my ten-year-old Chacos from college for going out and my Brooks Beast shoes for running, since my feet are flatter than a Nutella crepe.

Well, about halfway into my deployment, Justin and Shekinah dialed me up on FaceTime (we weren't exactly "roughing it" compared to my brothers over in Afghanistan) and said they wanted to get me some Nike swag for my birthday, probably because they pitied my situation, being away from Stacy for so long. I assumed they were going to get me a few shirts or maybe one pair of outlet kicks or something. But they let me literally scroll through the entire Nike store online and pick out whatever I wanted, in any color and in any quantity—a Nike blank check. I couldn't believe what I was experiencing. To Justin, it didn't cost him anything, as he had more credit to the store than he could ever use himself. But to me, this was one of the richest, most generous experiences I had ever had. They also offered to get some stuff for Stacy and ship it to her in the States. All in all, I think I might have picked out thirty-five pairs of shoes, ten hoodies, and other miscellaneous Dri-FIT items.

I got pairs of Jordan 1s, Air Max 1s, Air Max 97s, Nike SBs, Kobe lows, Jordan 13s, and many others, half of which I could never pull off as a white dude with a goofy military haircut. I basically picked out what I thought looked cool because I had no idea what I was looking at. This was the most generosity I had ever experienced outside of my parents repairing my '08 Honda Civic back to back to back in college when I blew out a head gasket three different times. Justin and Shekinah shipped all the gear to the States so it would be waiting for me when I got back from deployment.

When I returned from Romania, after Stacy and I got—ahem—reacquainted, I finally saw the towering piles of sneaker boxes and apparel bags and felt like a Cajun at a crawfish boil; I couldn't get enough. For some reason, the combination of the different styles, colorways (retail term for color variations), and collaborations of the sneakers instantly made me interested in learning about them and getting more. I have an obsessive personality as it is, so Stacy was not surprised when I dove into researching this new subculture. I'm not saying it's healthy; it's just what happened.

Getting thirty-five new pairs of shoes is obviously

overkill, and I could never wear that many, so I gave some of the kicks and hoodies to my buddies who wore the same size. Still, I was stacked for life, assuming I didn't horizontally outgrow the pieces of apparel (spoiler alert: I did). Like all my other hobbies, I immediately took to the internet to research more about my newfound interest. After thoroughly exploring sneaker Twitter and Instagram and watching every episode of Complex's *Sneaker Shopping* with Joe La Puma, I realized there was a whole world of sneakerheads who were into sneakers for buying, selling, and trading. Once I saw some of the profits I could make on certain sneakers, I was all in. So, as of this writing, I have only been interested in sneakers for about five years, but I learned a lot in a relatively short amount of time and count myself as an above-average fan of the sneaker world.

For some reason, the combination of the different styles, colorways, and collaborations of the sneakers instantly made me interested in learning about them and getting more.

Like many others, you may be flabbergasted at the sticker price or street value of some of these sneakers or designer pieces. I don't think it's strange for you to question why a pair of sneakers could be worth more than your Mercedes G-Class wagon payment or how a hoodie with a red rectangle in the middle of it could cost you more than a trip to London. The world freaked out in April 2019 when I posted a pic of Pastor John Gray donning the extremely coveted Nike Air Yeezy 2 Red Octobers, selling at the time in resale markets for more than $5,600.[1] And people struggled to comprehend my July 2019 post of Pastor Troy Gramling wearing the sought-after Supreme x Louis Vuitton box logo T-shirt, valued at more than $1,500 at the time.[2] It's a white tee with a logo on it. The average person may at least raise an eyebrow to the whole concept and wonder how we got here.

I honestly didn't know about the high-fashion designer world until I started PnS. That's partly why PreachersNSneakers created such a stir, because unsuspecting followers of these leaders of the faith were getting a first look at what this stuff was actually worth and were forced to wrestle with how they felt about it and why they felt that way. I imagine a lot of you just thought that these guys were trying to look "hip," and you never gave much thought to the price tag. "How could a pair of sneakers be worth so much?" you may ask now. Well, I'm about to tell you about one of my favorite hobbies. Be careful: you might just get hooked too.

The retail sneaker market worldwide was valued at more than $58 billion in 2018.[3] That's retail only. Sneakerheads have created an entirely different footwear economy: resale. The resale market is projected to be more than $6 billion globally by 2025.[4] The thing about sneakers is that some pairs are more limited in quantity, harder to find, or limited regionally, which drives up the demand and, concurrently, the amount owners are willing to accept to part with the sought-after kicks.

The retail sneaker market worldwide was more than $58 billion in 2018. That's retail only. Sneakerheads have created an entirely different footwear economy: resale.

On average, most new pairs of sneakers come out as a general release in "full family sizing." Basically, the company creates thousands of pairs in every size so that whoever wants to buy the sneakers can (in theory). There are other sneakers, however, that are more revered and sought after, of which the manufacturer will only make a limited number. Michael Jordan's original set of Player Exclusive "PE" shoes will get rereleased in different color combinations (colorways) that will often generate a different amount of hype depending on how rare or attractive that specific shoe is. Pair a new colorway with a collaboration with a current artist, brand, or athlete, and that drives up the anticipation and demand for the kicks even more. Some examples are Pharrell Williams's collaboration with Adidas and Supreme's with Nike. And, of course, Kanye West and Adidas created the billion-dollar Yeezy brand. The esteemed rapper Travis Scott has recently released numerous pairs of Nikes with his own specific designs that have instantly sold out online and in stores, causing the price to spike in the resale market.

Because you had to get lucky or stand in line for days to be able to purchase these limited sneaks, true sneaker fanatics and "hypebeasts" (basically people who want to be seen wearing the most coveted fashion/streetwear pieces) are willing to pay a premium to buy and wear them. Travis has even made certain pairs only available to friends and family (F&F), which skyrockets their market value.

On a recent trip to New York to interview Pastor David Nasser, I stopped into one of the most well-known sneaker boutiques in the world, Stadium Goods. Their whole business is to buy, consign, and sell limited-edition sneakers at a premium to those looking for the most exclusive kicks in the game. They're also somewhat of a free museum of sneakers that most people would never be able to see in their everyday lives. While I was there, they had one pair of purple F&F Jordan 4s that were designed by Travis Scott—super-rare. Their list price was $27,500. They also had a pair of the sought-after Eminem x Carhartt x Air Jordan 4s going for $20,000. Eventually I got to see, arguably, the grail of all grails: the Nike Air Mags, modeled after the famous self-lacing kicks Marty McFly wore in the film *Back to the Future Part II*. Their price? Fifty. Thousand. Dollars. For a pair of shoes!

Not only is the resale market itself blowing up, but the events surrounding sneakers are massive as well. Sneaker Con, for example, is a colossal gathering of fellow sneaker fanatics that happens in major cities across the world. Celebrities, sneaker brands, and fans all come together and interact for a couple of days to buy, trade, and flex the most hyped-up kicks. Often these events, where literally millions of dollars change hands, attract more than ten thousand people.[5] There are even celebrities within the sneaker resale culture—because why not? These include guys like Jaysse Lopez (Two Js Kicks), who once was homeless and now runs an almost $25 million sneaker resale shop in Vegas called Urban Necessities.[6] He's famous for a lot of things, but on YouTube, he has scores of videos of walking around Sneaker Con events and spending hundreds of thousands in cash on sneakers for him, his wife, and his store. Then there are other more content-focused players in the sneaker world who are celebrities in their own right. Guys like Jacques Slade, Seth Fowler, and my personal favorite, Brad Hall. These guys make a living off of literally unboxing and reviewing sneakers on YouTube.

I got to see, arguably, the grail of all grails: the Nike Air Mags, modeled after the famous self-lacing kicks Marty McFly wore in the film *Back to the Future Part II*. Their price? Fifty. Thousand. Dollars. For a pair of shoes!

For the Normal McNormalsons, outside of Sneaker Con and similar events, like ComplexCon, those in search of limited sneaks use platforms like StockX, GOAT, and eBay to buy/sell their prized possessions. StockX and GOAT are essentially stock markets of things where buyers set a bid price and sellers set an ask. You can either pay the price of someone's ask or set a bid if you're only willing to buy at a certain price. Once there is a match between buyer and seller, the seller sends the unworn kicks and box to a verification facility, and the buyer sends funds to escrow. Once the kicks are verified as authentic and sent to the buyer, the transaction is complete—all for a transaction fee. At scale, this quite literally creates a stock market–type environment for footwear, designer clothing, and other collectibles. eBay is still a heavily used option, but the purchase is riskier because you don't get to verify the kicks before buying. To date, StockX is where I have sourced most of my market data for the shoes the pastors wear.

Some of the most popular shoes featured on PreachersNSneakers are the Off-White collaboration with Jordan Brand. Off-White is a brand founded by the Illinois-born designer Virgil Abloh, who has an immense following in the fashion and streetwear world. He may be most well known for creating the minimalist branding that uses quotations and basic descriptors on clothing and furniture. Basically, he puts the words *hat* on a hat and *shirt* on a shirt and charges $300 for the apparel. Yes, it's an insane amount, but people pay it. Back to Jordan Brand: Virgil did a collaboration with the company to bring his signature style to ten of the most iconic Nike and

Jordan shoes. He used his signature quotation branding and also redesigned the kicks to look deconstructed, with some elements of the shoes barely hanging on by a thread. He also added a plastic hang tag that still draws debate about whether you're supposed to keep it on or not, much like the sticker on New Era 59FIFTY hats.

This first set of ten sneakers dropped on a single day in 2018 with extremely limited quantities and immediately sold out. I distinctly remember sitting in my office at my miserable corporate property management job, refreshing the Nike SNKRS app in hopes of securing just one pair. By some divine sneaker miracle, I actually got lucky and was able to buy the Off-White x Air Jordan 1s in the iconic Chicago (red and white) colorway. I paid $190 for them, plus shipping. The next week, I sold those same sneakers for more than $1,300 on StockX. This felt almost like free money. I quite literally lifted a single finger to buy and sell these shoes and made an almost 700 percent return. It was a double-edged sword looking back, though, because had I held on to those shoes, they'd now attract around a $4,000 to $5,000 price tag. After I realized that I could make real money on kicks, I was hooked on buying and reselling. It seemed like a no-brainer.

The immense hype and huge resale prices in the sneaker game have, in turn, created a great entrepreneurial activity for those of us who try to work side hustles. You can look up Benjamin Kickz, who got überfamous for being a teenager making a fortune from reselling sneakers to celebrities.[7] He was consistently featured in DJ Khaled's Snapchat as his exclusive "sneaker plug"—basically a connection for rare sneakers. There are big bucks to be made selling these shoes if you pay attention to the market, get lucky, and have your fulfillment logistics in order.

I realize this was a lot of information you probably didn't ask for, and I am by no means an expert, nor have I ever claimed to be, but having a little context makes it easier to understand my platform. For passersby, it can look like I am implying that the pastors actually paid the listed amount for the shoes. I have from the beginning never claimed to know how these guys and girls acquired the kicks; all I can show is what they are worth today. Some of my critics have a problem with me posting the resale value, saying, "pOSt ThE rEtAIl PrICE. tHiS is FaKE nEWz." But this brings up a fair question: Is something worth what someone else paid for it or what someone else is *willing* to pay for it?

I have from the beginning never claimed to know how these guys and girls acquired the kicks; all I can show is what they are worth today.

If you have a new pair of shoes that someone is willing to pay $1,000 for today and you instead choose to wear those shoes, forgoing the $1,000 cash, are you out $1,000 or just the $160 you paid for them retail? In my opinion, the answer is the former. From a cash-flow standpoint, yes, you are technically out only the $160. But with markets like StockX and GOAT, where you can sell your shoes today for the resale value, then if you say that you would rather wear the shoes, you are essentially wearing $1,000 shoes, a frivolous act to many.

What about if someone gave you a mint-condition, first-edition holographic Charizard Pokémon card—can't believe I'm mentioning freaking Pokémon again—and you saw that someone else was willing to pay you the $55,000 that it's going for (look it up; this is a real thing), yet you decided to keep the card and play with it. Was that card a $55,000 card or just worth the $5 that the pack cost you at the store?[8] Many people—myself included—see sneakers through this lens. You're giving up actual market value in order to wear them. Or in a more extreme case, if you were selling your house, would you sell it at the same price you paid for it? Hopefully not, because there is a market for houses. So if you bought your house in Austin for $300,000 twenty years ago, and now that house has appreciated in value to $1.2 million because it's in a desirable area and because the Austin housing market is insane to begin with, do you have a house worth $300,000 or $1.2 million? It's no different for sneakers, especially now that you know the market exists.

I'm a *yuge* fan of sneakers. I think they are one of the coolest hobbies right now because so much history, creativity, and technology goes into the culture. I'm no exception either—there's a reason the retail and resale markets are growing year over year. Many others love this world too. I get why churchgoers and their pastors are into it and absolutely don't denounce anyone for being interested in and devoting dollars to buying kicks. Understanding this world allows you to further appreciate the PreachersNSneakers discussion because there are meaningful dollar signs attached to the sneakers.

I do think it's worth discussing what our footwear and appearance—as well as our overall obsession with *things* as a Christian culture—communicate to others. Hobbies and interests aren't bad, obviously, but when a hobby or interest progressively becomes your god or causes others to envy you or feel less than, it's time to die to yourself and ask tough questions about its place in your heart. I have to do this constantly and am always at risk of propping up things as a god. Time after time—shocker alert—they are an incredibly miserable god to follow.

Discussion Questions

1. What's your stance on Christians owning sneakers worth more than the retail price? Does it matter?
2. How's your relationship with the hobbies and/or things you own? What helps you prevent these from owning you?
3. Culturally, how does consumerism play a role in the Christian church today?

Chapter Six

REGISTERED FLEX OFFENDERS

Are Your Lifestyle Posts a Sin?

The chilling February cold of New York City rushed right to our bones as we stepped out of the completely custom, matte-gray Ford Raptor truck worth more than $100,000. Stacy and I were filled with uncertainty about and anticipation for the moment we were about to step into. We walked around the corner to a decrepit-looking door that, to passersby, would seem like any other shoddy apartment or utility maintenance entrance. Standing right outside was a lone security guard, wearing a big-city peacoat that could have engulfed the four of us due to the size required to cover his cliché bouncer build. He made Pastor Keith Craft from Elevate Life Church look like a scrawny ball boy. The security guard inspected our IDs, taking a second look at Stacy's, because she still looks seventeen and is used to being carded for even the airplane exit row. He eventually allowed us to pass, and we entered the pitch-black hallway. There was a bright neon light at the opposite end, a glimmering outline of the greatest basketball star to ever play, Michael Jordan in his classic Jumpman pose. This is when the sneaker fanboy in me started to freak.

Justin and Shekinah Holiday had somehow convinced Justin's teammate Carmelo Anthony to allow them to bring along their two noncelebrity friends to his ultraexclusive Super Bowl party. Melo is a four-time Olympian and scoring machine in the NBA, so this was like a movie. After walking past the massive Jumpman logo, we turned the corner and were greeted by a theater-sized screen, a Vegas-style buffet, and blaring hip-hop from a live DJ. Melo and his wife, La La, stood up and greeted us as if we were all just at a normal watch party. The entire 2017 New York Knicks team was sitting on plush couches, focused on the now-infamous battle between the New England Patriots and the Atlanta Falcons. We eventually found seats between Joakim Noah and Kristaps Porzingis and paused to take in the super-normal situation. After a brief thirty seconds of appreciation, I took out my phone and immediately started showing the world how totally normal and chill I was among these towering titans of the game.

For a mega-average, mediocre-skilled dude from Louisiana, I've been able to experience some pretty unique VIP experiences, none of which I earned or deserved. As I mentioned in my note on sneakers, one of my best friends in the world is NBA shooting guard Justin Holiday. Throughout our friendship, he has selflessly hooked my wife and me up out of the goodness of his heart. For one, he's given me access to NBA locker rooms, practice facilities, super-fresh hotels, and amazing seats for as many of his games as we could make it to, free of charge. I've been able to shoot around in the Bulls' practice court, drive Justin's decked-out Ford Raptor into the Madison Square Garden (MSG) players' entrance, and dap up some of the greatest players in the game, like Steph Curry and Jimmy Butler. We've even gotten access to the fully stocked family suites that usually only family members get to enjoy, complete with open bar (of Cokes!) and immaculate spreads of free food. Not only that, but Justin has brought us along for exclusive events off the court, like sitting in the owner's box at MSG for a Lumineers concert, where we shared sushi with NBA legend Phil Jackson and rubbed elbows with other New York City elites.

For a mega-average, mediocre-skilled dude from Louisiana, I've been able to experience some pretty unique VIP experiences, none of which I earned or deserved.

These were once-in-a-lifetime experiences. That's not lost on me. Hardly anyone gets to see the inner workings of professional sports. I count myself incredibly lucky to have such a close relationship with someone in a small subset of the sports world who is willing to share the spoils of his hard work and dedication.

Maybe basketball doesn't mean anything to you. What about comedy? I consider humor the most spiritual of services you can provide to someone. Everyone thinks they're funny, but only a few can consistently bring me to laughter. Throughout the life of PreachersNSneakers, I have been able to meet some pretty incredible comedians and actors, including the Hollywood types. One of my favorites, who also happened to write the foreword to this book, is actor, comedian, and sultan of sarcasm Joel McHale. Joel reached out to me during my eight seconds of fame, and we struck up a great friendship via DM. As he mentioned in the super-subtle foreword, you probably know Joel from his recurring roles on *Community*, *The Soup*, and *Card Sharks*. He's also had cameo appearances on pretty much every current sitcom and late-night show out there. Of course, his new career highlight may be writing the foreword to this book. Hmm . . .

What you probably don't know is that Joel and his wife, Sarah, are Christians and some of the most generous people in the game. Up to this point, I have had really nothing to offer Joel other than poor attempts at jokes, but he has selflessly given Stacy and me so much. Not only did he blast my content across his platforms and share it with his celeb friends, but he also agreed to be a guest on my podcast. As part of recording the podcast, Joel invited Stacy and me, sight unseen, to his Hollywood Hills mansion. We had never met in person before, but he let us just roll up to his crib. We could have easily been murderers, but thankfully both parties turned out to be normalish people.

Joel welcomed us in, cooked for us, and spent several hours talking to Stacy and me, getting to know about our lives. After recording the podcast episode, he sent us home with multiple bottles of wine . . . er . . . I mean Pepsi. Most people never get a behind-the-scenes look at a megaceleb-rity, but I did, and I was dying to let the world see. While I tried to play it cool, like I had been there before and was not starstruck when meeting and interacting with celebs, I thought this experience was the dopest thing ever. Of course I wanted everyone in my circle to know. Admittedly, I made a few posts on PreachersNSneakers IG stories because I couldn't help but show how cool my new influencer life was.

Admittedly, I made a few posts on PreachersNSneakers IG stories because I couldn't help but show how cool my new influencer life was.

Have you ever had an amazing experience, vacation, or celebrity interaction? What is the first thing you would do if you got to sit in those free NBA courtside seats or backstage greenrooms? Like most normal people in a social media-obsessed world, you would probably pepper the gram with your photos, vid-eos, and stories of how cool it all was and how it was just a typical part of your life. And that's what I did. I did not hesitate to spam my followers with more pics of me in the suite or on the court or backstage. I absolutely felt like the world should see how cool my life was and assumed that people would genuinely be happy for me and not stumble or be jealous because that is totally how I always feel for others when they get something good 😖.

In Christian circles, I wonder how much thought is put into what we post. I think most people probably run their posts through the initial filter of "Is this a photo of me doing a keg stand or wearing a tiny swimsuit? No? Then I'm probably good." I wonder what your pastors would say if you told them that their dope vacation or celebrity pics were causing you to stumble. Would your concern be treated the same as if they'd posted pictures of their hot wives in bikinis? Do we really even care if someone in digital land can't handle a "harmless" picture of our free ranch-house trip? Shouldn't people just be happy for us if we get the rare treat to go on a vacation? If not, what really is the difference between causing someone to lust after a body versus lust after our opportunities or circumstances?

Go to any of the profiles of the PnS-regular pastors and you will see, among their well-curated preaching pics, photos of them rubbing shoulders with the biggest celebrities in the world. You can see Carl Lentz hooping with Drake, Rich Wilkerson Jr. on a FaceTime call with the Biebs, or Craig Groeschel and his chiseled jawline hanging out with Kanye at his ranch in Wyoming. You can also see them on frequent, exquisite beach and mountain vacations, seemingly always bringing a professional photographer along to capture those precious candid moments in the chalet.

On my cleverly named podcast, *The Preachers NSneakers Podcast*, I hosted my pastor-buddy Jonathan Pokluda (JP), whom I've mentioned before, to talk about the prosperity gospel and Christians' use of social media. If you haven't already, I encourage you to listen to all of this episode because it is chock-full of wisdom and truth (from JP, not from me). During our conversation, JP highlighted the dangers of social media and what we choose to post as believers:

> **JP:** Do you think jealousy is a sin?
>
> **BK:** (long, awkward pause trying to figure out if this is a trick question) I think envy is a sin, yeah. Yeah, jealousy is a sin.
>
> **JP:** Yeah, yeah, without a doubt jealousy is a sin. Envy is a sin. And what's interesting about social media is so much of what we post is in an effort to make people jealous.
>
> **BK:** Right.
>
> **JP:** And I think we're really gonna have to give an answer to that. I think that's something that we've been, really, not careful on. I'll speak for myself specifically, like when I go on vacation, you know, it's like, "Look where I'm at, look where I got to go." . . . What I'm doing is I'm just causing someone to stumble. . . . I'm trying to make someone jealous of me. And that's a sin.[1]

Why are we so determined to let the world see into our beautiful lives? Is it to normalize us as regular people? Is it to encourage others to take time to recharge, rest, and reflect? Or, deep down, might we juuuuusst enjoy the idea of our followers thinking we've got a pretty dope life? I wonder why the pastor community hasn't expressed much thought on this concept. Even if you don't think you are purposely trying to make others envy your life, do you agree that there is some element of what Kort Marley calls "Social Comparison Syndrome"? In his book *Navigating the Digital Sea: Gospel Guidance for Social Media*, Marley described this as "the unhealthy habit of online comparison that creates bitterness, disdain, or pride."[2]

Why are we so determined to let the world see into our beautiful lives?

Numerous studies explore the effects of consuming social media every day and social media's connection to depression and anxiety. While many variables are at play, one 2019 study of 3,826 Canadian adolescents showed that increased hours spent on social media led to significant increases in feelings of depression and anxiety.[3] If you agree with the data, it seems we are, at best, complicit in causing some form of depression and anxiety in others; at worst, we are literally causing our brothers and sisters in Christ to sin. Do you care? Do I care? If so, what can we do better?

So, the lifestyle pics and celebrity flexes are one

thing, but what about Christians performing overtly "Christian" acts for the gram? Along with immaculately curated photos, we have a generation of pastors and Christian performers that puts (commonly private) Christian acts on display. I've recently been struggling with one element of this: livestreaming prayers. I'm not talking about a thirty-second clip of an introductory prayer from a YouTube sermon, but five minutes of emotionally praying for all the world to see. The easiest target for this is DeVon Franklin, the famed prosperity preacher/motivational speaker who is married to *Cousin Skeeter* star Meagan Good. On a weekly basis, he hosts a livestream of himself praying on his Instagram. This is not a guided prayer for others but a video of only him praying and tons of onlookers commenting. How do we align this with verses like Matthew 6:1, which literally says "not to practice your righteousness in front of others to be seen"? For Christians, does this apply to social media or no?

When we record something or start an IG live, we know our followers are going to see it. We know that others are going to have the ability to like, share, and comment on that piece of content. Should we consider that before we jump into a passionate intercession for the day's topic? Obviously, Jesus never commented on topics like social media, but He did care about hearts and intent. If the verses do apply, we all—celeb pastors included—need to take a major inventory of what we are releasing into the Zuckersphere. If they don't apply, then what does "And when you pray, do not be like the hypocrites, for they love to pray standing in the synagogues and on the street corners to be seen by others" actually mean (Matt. 6:5)? My fear is that we have ignored the warnings of Jesus when it comes to what we create and how we spend our time online and have replaced them with a desire to impress others.

My fear is that we have ignored the warnings of Jesus when it comes to what we create and how we spend our time online and have replaced them with a desire to impress others.

Look, I agree that a healthy prayer life is massively important to our spiritual journeys and growth. I absolutely want to know that my pastor, especially, is taking everything to God in the pursuit of leading our church. I guess I just question the purpose of sharing a well-curated photo or video of you praying. To me, such a post risks being more about image than about an intimate relationship with your Creator. Jesus gave further instruction about our prayer lives in Matthew 6:6–8:

> "But when you pray, go into your room, close the door and pray to your Father, who is unseen. Then your Father, who sees what is done in secret, will reward you. And when you pray, do not keep on babbling like

> pagans, for they think they will be heard because of their many words. Do not be like them, for your Father knows what you need before you ask him."

Jesus wants us to have no hint of being righteous for the approval of others.

Jeremy Ham wrote a helpful article about this tension back in 2011 in which he made this conclusion:

> Prayer is a vital aspect of Christian living [1 Thess. 5:16–18]. . . . We should work toward a continual state of prayer unto God—praying constantly and always being mentally prepared to pray. Furthermore, we should . . . rely upon God to meet all our needs. We have no reason to worry when we have a God who cares about His people [Phil. 4:6].
>
> We can, indeed, pray everywhere, as long as we are praying for the right reasons. Praying for prideful reasons only receives earthly rewards. In everything we do, our focus should be on Christ, not ourselves. Jesus Christ has done so much for us, and the proper response for the gift of salvation is to show our love to Him and put Him first in our lives. As an added benefit, focusing on Christ will lay up treasures in heaven.[4]

So yes, of course the answer is that it's all about intent. What about perceived intent when you're a massive public figure who influences millions of people? Should we as fellow believers care about how you are portraying your spiritual life? I struggle to understand what the benefit is of putting on a spiritual show for millions of social media followers. Maybe the extent to which it influences others to pray outweighs the risk of looking like you are practicing righteousness in public.

I know it's exhausting to question the intent of every type of social post out there in the Christian world. I don't really love doing it either, but if it gets us even an inch closer to more carefully considering what we post, is it worth questioning? Or should we just accept the status quo?

There are the emotional social media prayers, and then there are the super-public spectacles of charitable giving, usually around Christmas. This probably applies more to Christian public figures than the average person with three hundred followers. There is a rising trend of pastors making their churches' giving practices known to the world. At the tail end of 2019, Transformation Church pastor Michael Todd did a sermon series called Crazy Faith. In the series, he called up various people—singles and families—and described a need that they had expressed previously. Then he handed them a box or an envelope that they would open to unveil a check or car keys or new drums or whatever. Over the course of the sermon series, Transformation Church gave away $1.2 million from its missions fund. The church gave not only to individuals but also to numerous national organizations. That is a ton of money and was incredibly generous.[5]

The reason my account blew up in the first place is because I tend to lean on the cynical side, and I posed questions that many others were thinking but never knew how—or wanted—to ask. This is something I'm actively wrestling with, but bear with me. Could Transformation Church have given out these donations within the privacy of its church community? Did the church really need to broadcast this giving for the world to see?

The reason my account blew up in the first place is because I tend to lean on the cynical side, and I posed questions that many others were thinking but never knew how—or wanted—to ask.

As of this writing, that video has more than five hundred thousand views on YouTube. Here's the church leadership's explanation for why they gave this money away:

> This is all about inspiring belief. Our mission is to represent God to people. We want to see their lives changed, but oftentimes, people have tangible needs that need to be met, and it's like you can talk to me about your big God when you help me with this hunger issue or help me with this housing issue.[6]

Seems like fair reasoning and a genuine desire to show people how God can meet real needs. Would it change anything if I told you that Pastor Mike Todd signed a book deal around that same time? When his maiden voyage into writing, titled *Relationship Goals*, released months later, it immediately landed on the *New York Times* Best Sellers list and remained there for fourteen weeks straight.

At the time, I actually shared the video of Pastor Todd giving away the money and cars as something to be praised: a pastor and church actually putting real dollars toward what they said they were about instead of just vaguely talking about how God helps you in times of need. But was the giving truly about inspiring belief after all? It's impossible to tell, but this is the danger of using your platform as a spiritual leader to also build your personal brand. It's easy for critics like me to say, "Well, yeah, you gave away $1.2 mil, but you also made mainstream headlines just in time for the release of your first book, which is now immensely successful. What's the deal with that?"

You may be thinking, *Okay, that's such a freaking stretch. Can't churches just do nice things without everyone assuming ill intent?* Sure they can. But they chose to release their good works into the ether. Can I not also ask the questions that may help others with discerning what is good and right versus what is being abused or misused? Can you blame me and many others for at least raising an eyebrow after years and years of embezzlement and scandal within Christian megachurches?

Rich Wilkerson Jr. and his wildly popular VOUS Church took a page out of the same publicity playbook when they went around to different organizations in Miami, giving away money in time for Christmas. While their giving wasn't near the size and scope of Transformation's, VOUS did give $60,000 to various organizations that benefit foster care and other young people in Miami.[7] The $60,000 was generous, sure, but they filmed their team handing over this obscenely oversized novelty check to the head of each organization, which seemed to create pressure for the recipients to provide a reaction for the camera. What was the point of filming and sharing this video? Could it be that publicizing how your donations are being used is a pretty effective tool for inspiring year-end giving?

Going back to Matthew 6, Jesus literally said that when we give to the needy, we shouldn't announce it like hypocrites do in order to be honored by men (v. 2). He also commanded that we not let our left hand know what our right hand is doing so that the giving may be in secret, because that's what God will reward (v. 3). Essentially, He was saying to not do any of this for show. Again, it's impossible to judge the hearts of the aforementioned guys and their platforms, but it's also impossible to deny the publicity and fundraising benefits of showing the world what and how they gave. What if you genuinely do want to help others and also know that it will bring about great publicity for the book or conference tickets you need to sell? This is, at least, something worth considering.

I do understand why many of these churches are moving toward publicizing their generosity and community activities. Our culture has basically forced them to. If you read through the comments on my account, many followers ask the question, "Why would they buy X or Y when they could've used that money to give to the poor?" On the opposite end, there are also people—like me—who, when churches do share some of the things they are doing in the community, immediately spring to say something like, "Oh, they're just doing this to pat themselves on the back or generate donations." The social media community has created quite a catch-22 for modern-day pastors: damned if you do, damned if you don't.

I do think we ought to push more of the attention toward the God that church serves and the community being helped and less toward the guy or girl leading that organization or movement.

I do think we ought to push more of the attention toward the God that church serves and the community being helped and less toward the guy or girl leading that organization or movement. I think fighting against vanity and trying to display wisdom instead of creating catchy visuals and elevating the organization's figurehead would truly benefit the cause of Christ. Any chance we have of living out John 3:30, which says, "He must become greater; I must become less," is time and effort well spent.

To be clear, this whole chapter is me pointing the mirror at myself. Over the past year, while I haven't posted much on my personal socials, I have still spent an obscene amount of time online, specifically on Instagram. My iPhone tracks this, and I have averaged five to nine freaking hours a day between IG, Twitter, and Messages without even trying. I just checked, and I picked up my phone more than three hundred times yesterday. While we need to address the heart behind why we post what we post, I need to repent of the legitimate addiction I have to perusing the virtual world in search of new content or inspiration for something to comment or share, always on the hunt for that small dopamine hit. I absolutely use that time to compare my life, platform, and notoriety to that of others. I (for sure) measure my fourteen chins against the guy with abs and what my family looks like compared to complete strangers. I feel immense depression on some days when I see that a friend just got a sick new job or started a cool company or bought a four-thousand-square-foot home at the country club that his parents helped fund. It gives me pure anxiety to see others seemingly pursue their dreams while I feel stuck, still trying to figure out what to do with my life.

Not only do I have to repent of my need to compare

my life to the lives of others, but I also have to repent of making an idol out of likes, comments, and followers. I get so much fake value out of having a couple hundred thousand followers or having a post get ten thousand likes. All of that is meaningless, yet I often put much more effort into getting responses online than responding to the One who died for my sins.

In his letter to the Corinthian church way back in the day, Paul described the characteristics of love.

> Love is patient, love is kind. It does not envy, it does not boast, it is not proud. It does not dishonor others, it is not self-seeking, it is not easily angered, it keeps no record of wrongs. Love does not delight in evil but rejoices with the truth. It always protects, always trusts, always hopes, always perseveres. (1 Cor. 13:4–7)

I imagine this has to apply to the actions, intentions, and responses we show online.

All of us need to consider why we post what we post. How can we check the heart behind what and why we post? Just as someone's appearance can cause someone else to stumble, so can our tropical vacation pics. Whether we think it's actually a sin or not to post that pic of our new house or Range Rover or whatever, what if we took a second to think about why we really want to share our posts with the world? We might be surprised by what we discover.

Discussion Questions

1. How have you committed registered flex offenses? Would it be worth taking a personal social media inventory?
2. How's your heart with what you post? Do you love the idea of people thinking your life is awesome?
3. How should church leaders use social media platforms?

Chapter Seven

WOKE WORSHIPERS AND POLITICKING PASTORS

Should Faith Leaders Use Platforms for Political Influence?

Imagine you're one of the most popular hypepriests or suited-up megapastors in the game. You have a coveted blue check and a million Instagram followers, fifty thousand Twitter followers, and two million YouTube subscribers. In these spaces, your adoring fans and church members can see you preaching invigorating sermon series in the language of the people, with relevant titles like 20/20 Vision and Secure the Bag or more self-helpy titles like Choosing Faith over Worry and Leveraging Your Future. Everyone says you're even better live, which is why thousands of committed members show up to your church each Sunday. Within those crowds are, inevitably, some of the wealthiest and most powerful people in the city—government leaders, business owners, athletes, and a smattering of millionaires. All of them look up to you for spiritual leadership and motivation. The phone in your pocket contains the personal contact information for some of the most notable Americans. You're also probably one of Justin Bieber's fifteen personal pastors, because who isn't at this point?

While you may have never sought out any of this when you first got the call to ministry, you now undeniably have a platform of, perhaps, global influence. With this immense success you can shape the opinions of thousands. In addition to money and fame, you also have legitimate power over your staff, your congregation, and those in the Twittersphere. These three highly valued cultural currencies act like a dinner bell for hungry politicians. Political leaders seek you out, snap a postable photo with you, listen to your concerns, and seem to care about what matters to you. In reality, they are earning your trust because they need all of your fans and followers and church members and celebrity mentees to vote and advocate for them. To a parishioner, you are a pastor, but to a politician, you are an influential tool (changing my LinkedIn title to this).

To a parishioner, you are a pastor, but to a politician, you are an influential tool.

This story, or some version of it, has been repeated again and again since at least the late twentieth century in America. Take Pastor Robert Jeffress, for example. He felt called to ministry at the ripe age of sixteen—you know, the age when everybody figures out exactly what they want to do with their lives. After college and seminary, he bounced around at a few congregations in Texas before landing a gig as the senior pastor of the fourteen-thousand-member First Baptist Church of

Dallas. In Texas, to be a pastor is to be almost equal to the local politicians. As a leader of such an impressionable and devout audience, you have influence beyond your comprehension.

Pastor Bob's good fortune has resulted in book deals, a nationwide television ministry, and radio opportunities, as well as becoming a spiritual adviser for President Donald Trump. You will find him on many weeknights in front of a camera as a paid contributor for Fox News, offering hot takes on culture war debates, stumping for the president, or explaining how the Democrats are destroying America's moral fabric.

None of this will surprise you if you attend Jeffress's church. Services there regularly feature theological heavyweights, including Fox News host Sean Hannity, conservative radio shock jock Todd Starnes, and former Trump White House press secretary Sarah Huckabee Sanders. His church's choir even performed an original hymn titled "Make America Great Again" for the president at a veterans concert in Washington, DC.[1]

Jack Graham, pastor of Prestonwood Baptist Church in Dallas, not only has been a Trump supporter but also wrote an opinion piece for the *Dallas Morning News* in which he said,

> Those of us, especially evangelicals, who care about the sanctity of human life, will have to redouble our efforts to make sure unborn children have the right to live. I'm

> thankful that President Trump has proven a reliable partner in this fight. . . . The better question is not why an evangelical would support President Trump, but how is it possible for a Bible-believing evangelical to not support the most pro-life president in the history of the United States.[2]

To be clear, Jeffress and Graham are not the only religious leaders who have leveraged their spiritual authority for political influence. Lots of their fellow conservative Christians have become vocal and visible on the political scene, and for their endorsements, support, and public prayers, they have been rewarded handsomely with White House photo ops, exclusive listening sessions, and even presidential appointments. The religious roster on the Trump Train includes Guillermo Maldonado, Kenneth Copeland, Jentezen Franklin, Kari Jobe, and even Franklin Graham, the notable son of the late Billy Graham.

After South Carolina pastor and televangelist Mark Burns gained national recognition for his support of Donald Trump, he made his ambitions known by (unsuccessfully) running for Congress. Georgia pastor Jody Hice also ran for Congress as a Republican—and won. In a blink, he traded his pulpit for a campaign stump.

Of course, we must mention Trump's pastor in chief and PreachersNSneakers content gold mine, Paula White. She is a bona fide prosperity preacher who is often photographed in exquisite designer items. White also controversially divorced her second husband and married Jonathan Cain, keyboardist for the band Journey. A top spiritual adviser, she's been tied to financial disputes surrounding Without Walls, the church she once led with her former husband Randy White. She was also the subject of an inquiry by the United States Senate Committee on Finance (with whom she refused to cooperate)[3] and had some sort of interesting relationship with famed faith healer Benny Hinn.[4]

Apparently, President Trump reached out to White in 2002 after he saw her TV show,[5] and he flew her to Atlantic City for private meetings.[6] She's been credited with converting Trump to Christianity,[7] and she offered the prayer for his inaugural ceremony in 2017. President Trump appointed her to lead the White House's Faith and Opportunity Initiative, which coordinates political outreach to religious organizations and personalities. All of Paula White's newfound political power and influence started with her being a preacher.

Of course, conservative Christians aren't the only ones who struggle with partisan politicking. When Democratic politicians are on the campaign trail, they, too, regularly stop by left-leaning churches to deliver speeches and receive similar treatment from adoring masses. While their partisanship may receive less media attention, it still seems pretty overt. In 1995, when President Bill Clinton was fighting for his proposed budget, he invited more than a dozen progressive faith leaders to the White House for a special forty-five-minute meeting in the Oval Office. At the conclusion of their time together, the religious leaders gathered around the president, laid hands on him, and prayed that God would "make the president strong for the task" of budget negotiations.[8]

Similarly, President Obama led one of the most aggressive faith outreach efforts, both in his campaign and during his terms as president, in modern American history. In a *New York Times* article about President Obama's inaugural campaign, Laurie Goodstein wrote, "Campaign workers contacted individual ministers, even those they knew would not necessarily vote for Mr. Obama, and mailed copies of his speeches on faith and politics to thousands of them." The goal was to humanize him and show that he had a genuine faith, in hopes that opposing pastors would think twice before speaking out against him publicly.

> The campaign also visited about 10 Christian colleges in swing states, often staging events with Donald Miller, a bestselling author popular with younger evangelicals and an Obama supporter. And campaign workers organized more than 900 "American values house parties," in which Obama supporters invited members of their church to talk politics.[9]

Politicians on both sides know that pastors are the influential key to the Christian vote.

The lines between the Christian church and the public square have been noticeably blurred. For those who follow the news, it's getting harder and harder to tell the difference between politicians and preachers.

The lines between the Christian church and the public square have been noticeably blurred.

• • •

When I was growing up in the evangelical church in the 1990s, our family had a clear understanding of what being Christian meant politically. We supported the politicians who held to "Christian values," such as opposing abortion, gay marriage, big government, and religious censorship. These politicians, unsurprisingly, always ended up being Republican, so even though we wouldn't have stated it so clearly, the fix was in: to be Christian was to be Republican.

Most of my evenings were spent watching Fox News in front of our family's thirteen-inch TV/VCR combo that my parents "splurged" on one day at Sam's Club. Not to sound like a typical doctor's kid, but my dad was a doctor, so I'm still puzzled by how we couldn't even spring for a solid thirty-two-inch box like my homies had. This was the golden age of '90s television, so being forced to watch *Wishbone* and replays of *Swiss Family Robinson*—basically the only homeschool-appropriate programs at the time—on this tiny screen felt like mild torture. Regardless, my house was narrated by the likes of Bill O'Reilly or Greta Van Susteren, tsk-tsking the outrage flavor of the week. The more they spoke and the more I listened, the more livid we all grew at the "liberal agenda" that was threatening America.

The hypernegativity of cable news combined with a rethinking of how religion and politics should interact has made me somewhat averse to politics as an adult. I squirm when a pastor endorses any candidate, no matter the party. I'm uncomfortable with an organization called Evangelicals for Trump hosting campaign rallies in church sanctuaries with American flags draped over the baptistry.[10] And I don't like it when liberal politicians and preachers—who are admittedly less brazen but more pretentious—behave in similar ways. Connecting the faith I so strongly believe in with a political movement or party that I do not feel as strongly about feels like I am being forced into one of two groups of which I do not want to be a part.

I've met a lot of Christians who feel similarly. Millennials like me are the generation of religious deconstruction, often questioning and potentially casting out their parents' faith traditions. Along with an aversion to cheesy music and disingenuous personalities, my generation has grown weary of politics making its way into the pulpit, causing many millennials to leave the church altogether. Friends in my own circles are transitioning to a home-church model, where families meet exclusively with a small group of people in homes around town. There are a whole host of reasons why they are moving to this in droves, but the shift was partly to avoid the political smothering from traditional churches. Look up the history of Judah Smith's Churchome, and you'll find it pretty much started exactly that way.

Along with an aversion to cheesy music and disingenuous personalities, my generation has grown weary of politics making its way into the pulpit, causing many millennials to leave the church altogether.

The relationship between religious and political power brokers works out well for those directly involved. But the creeping allure of political power, much like money and fame, has had devastating effects on the American church. Church attendance is declining among almost every denomination and sect, and has been for some time. The decline is particularly steep among young people. When asked why they are leaving, many defectors cite religious partisanship. For example, a recent LifeWay Research poll reported that 70 percent of young adults who stopped attending church regularly said religious, ethical, or political beliefs led to their leaving the church. Twenty-five percent said they "disagreed with the church's stance on political/social issues."[11]

I'm not saying that pastors cannot voice wise counsel or comment on current political events. Without political engagement from pastors, there would be no civil rights movement. But there is a difference between politics and partisanship. The gospel has something to say to the political realm, but it should never bow to a political party and platform. "Jesus is Lord" is a powerful spiritual declaration, but it makes a terrible campaign slogan.

The issue here is not just about politics generally or even partisanship specifically. It is about the driving force that makes both of these run: power. Yes, I know that sounds a smidge dramatic, but bear with me. The Christian faith, along with its two testaments, says a thing or two about this.

Jesus addressed politically co-opted religious leaders of His day on multiple occasions in the Bible, and He was rarely flattering. Several times in the Gospel of Matthew, Jesus called them a "brood of vipers" and "hypocrites," which is probably not the best way to get invited to a state dinner. While the Bible promotes obedience to the government and political leaders through paying taxes and praying for those God has placed in leadership, we never find Jesus promoting, politicking, or stumping for a political leader. And you won't find any record of a prominent early Christian behaving in this way until a couple of centuries after the crucifixion. The gospel seeks to unite us to a Person, not a party, and I fear that many of those claiming to follow Christ are more worried about the latter than the former.

The gospel seeks to unite us to a Person, not a party, and I fear that many of those claiming to follow Christ are more worried about the latter than the former.

Many of us are as careless about our political engagement as these leaders are. Depending on how and where you grew up, you likely have a handful of issues that you support based on your faith. Whether those issues are religious freedom, pacifism, or pro-lifeism, you can list all of the reasons your position is moral. You can even quote a bunch of Bible verses to make your case. But this is where we often fall off the rails. These faithful positions harden into partisan activism, uncontrollable outrage, and fear—or even hatred—of others.

In his book *A Faith of Our Own: Following Jesus Beyond the Culture Wars*, Jonathan Merritt explored the negative effects of Christianity's fusion with partisanship, making this claim:

> Christians diminish God by aligning Him with partisan preferences. Baptizing complex party platforms with religious vernacular makes our position synonymous

> with God's position. . . . Whether intended or not, dragging partisan politics into the sanctuary scribbles "thus saith the Lord" across opinions. Once the association is made, those on the other side of the aisle are not merely mistaken; they are apostate.[12]

What does Merritt desire most for Christians and their relationship with politics?

> I long for more Christians to engage in the public square with the same integrity: resisting the pull of partisanship, standing courageously in the middle; speaking with love and mutual respect for those who claim other parties; clinging to the gospel, but not in a way that marginalizes listeners based on their political affiliations.[13]

Sounds about right.

Generations of Christians and skeptical nonbelievers have seen the way religion and politics have conspired over the last few decades and are rethinking the relationship. They don't want to withdraw from the public square, especially at a time when so much is at stake, but they are worried about the partisan captivity of many American churches, if not flat-out turned off by it. This new generation is voting their values . . . by walking away from Christian churches in record numbers. But I can't help thinking that it doesn't have to be this way.

By elevating a particular party, we risk the influence of our faith on others around us. This has been evident in past presidencies but most recently during the Trump era. Christians have had to choose whether to support a man with an immensely checkered, unrepentant past and present or denounce his character and thus alienate the majority on the right. In an article for the *Atlantic*, Peter Wehner broke this down:

> There's a very high cost to our politics for celebrating the Trump style, but what is most personally painful to me as a person of the Christian faith is the cost to the Christian witness. Nonchalantly jettisoning the ethic of Jesus in favor of a political leader who embraces the ethic of Thrasymachus and Nietzsche—might makes right, the strong should rule over the weak, justice has no intrinsic worth, moral values are socially constructed and subjective—is troubling enough.
>
> But there is also the undeniable hypocrisy of people who once made moral character, and especially sexual fidelity, central to their political calculus and who are now embracing a man of boundless corruptions. Don't forget: Trump was essentially named an unindicted co-conspirator ("Individual 1") in a scheme to make hush-money payments to a porn star who alleged she'd had an affair with him while he was married to his third wife, who had just given birth to their son.[14]

For a people who are called to "make disciples of all nations" (Matt. 28:19), limiting our reach to those who agree with our partisan political stance is hardly an effective strategy. If we truly care about spreading the gospel of Jesus to all people, where does allegiance to a party exist? What about a country itself? As a former officer of the US Marines, I have wrestled with the idea of having allegiance to a country while also trying to have allegiance to Jesus, a Jew from the Middle East. If the places and communities where we worship are deeply aligned to one political party or the other, does that risk becoming an idol itself and further detracting from our worship of God?

If the places and communities where we worship are deeply aligned to one political party or the other, does that risk becoming an idol itself and further detracting from our worship of God?

Back to Peter Wehner, who advocated for a new model in how Christians should approach politics:

> Evangelical Christians need another model for cultural and political engagement, and one of the best I am aware of has been articulated by the artist Makoto Fujimura, who speaks about "culture care" instead of "culture war."

> . . . What Fujimura is talking about is a set of sensibilities and dispositions that are fundamentally different from what we see embodied in many white evangelical leaders who frequently speak out on culture and politics . . . characterized by a commitment to grace, beauty, and creativity, not antipathy, disdain, and pulsating anger. It's the difference between an open hand and a mailed fist.[15]

I find myself, as I'm sure a lot of you do, somewhere in the middle of this. On one hand, I think it's ridiculous that pastors and churches can so adamantly stump for one political party/candidate or the other. The entire theme of this book is that we should elevate Jesus over everything and everyone. On the other hand, I do think there are real-life issues worth fighting for, which could easily lead to our wanting to see our guy or girl in office. The logic makes sense: if we care about an issue, and that candidate claims to also care about the issue, then we should want that candidate to win. However, the jump from advocating for someone who shares our values to using any and all platforms and opportunities to push that candidate into office, thereby alienating anyone who disagrees, is very quick. As imperfect followers of a perfect God, we need to fight for empathy and understanding but also know when to stand our ground. We are never promised an equilibrium on this tension in this life, but we should aspire to find as much balance as possible.

Discussion Questions

1. Do you think there is a place for political parties in a church context?
2. How have your political beliefs intertwined with your Christian walk?
3. How can the church love everyone from all sides while also advocating for justice, protecting the powerless, and promoting freedom to worship?

Chapter Eight

PURSUE YOUR PROMISED PURPOSE, PARTICULARLY PROVING YOUR PREDESTINATION

Can Self-Help and the Gospel Coexist?

You've felt it before. You're sitting in church, or at a conference or a Hillsong concert, and a relatively attractive dude is onstage, talking about some story from his life that he's about to relate to Habakkuk or something. At the beginning, you take everything in objectively, but after you've been sitting and listening for, like, thirty minutes, you build some type of short-term connection with the speaker. As he reaches the tail end of his sermon, he starts connecting the message to your life, your struggles. Somehow he becomes instantly more relatable, seemingly speaking to the very issue you're facing. You think, *Wait, is this dude giving me a word specifically from God right now?*

For some reason you now feel super-enthused with the Spirit, ready to run through a wall for Jesus. No amount of adversity or awkwardness and no number of social issues can keep you from going all-in for Christ. This time will be different. The pastor starts hitting you with a Mighty Ducks triple-deke combo of alliteration, like "Your path has been predestined to promise your purpose" or "You gotta be bodaciously bought into the burden to receive your blessing." No Scripture needed; you *feel* the Holy Spirit filling you up inside in a way you've never felt before. Surely this is God speaking to you, and not some skilled communicator playing into your senses.

Music starts playing from out of nowhere, and you immediately stand to your feet, lift your hands, and start saying, "*Yesssssss*," along with the other Anthropologie models around you. The dude onstage is now literally screaming, and you're all about it. This feels good; this must be good. Then the equally sexy young adult pastor gets up on the stage, asks you for some type of giving commitment, and abruptly tells you that the service is dismissed. Now it's over. There has been no real call to action other than to fund the church for next week and to pursue your dreams. It's time for you to go home and come down from this emotional dousing.

What did that service actually do for you? Sure, it was entertaining. Sure, it was motivating (to do what, though?). And, sure, it felt like nothing you've ever felt before in a church context; you were used to the suits, pews, grannies, and judgment of traditional church experiences. I get it. We need to reach "youths," as Schmidt from the comedy series *New Girl* says, but at what cost?

At the risk of sounding like a church curmudgeon, this is a pretty standard experience for metropolitan-area churchgoers these days. Gone are the days of a choir, a suited-up pastor, and random people sitting in velvet chairs onstage. No. Now it's a U2 incarnate worship band, perfectly placed LED wash lights, and a pastor who not only looks fresh but is a mix between Gary Vaynerchuk and Tony Robbins. He's motivating, edgy, and might even let a cussword slip if you're lucky. If you want to grow a congregation these days, this is the model you need for the programming. The *New York Times* described this model perfectly:

> Saving souls is a business like any other. Pastors today who want to start a ministry for those 40 and under follow a well-traveled path. First, they lease an old theater or club. Next, they find great singers and backup musicians. A fog machine on stage is nice. A church should also have a catchy logo or catchphrase that can be stamped onto merchandise and branded—socks, knit hats, shoes and sweatshirts. . . . And lastly, churches need a money app . . . to make it easy for churchgoers to tithe with a swipe on their smartphones.[1]

These churches will probably stay away from pain, suffering, and sin and focus more on your purpose, your blessing, and getting through your anxiety and/or depression. The pastors will talk about your dating and your finances, your friendships and your careers. You, you, you, you, you. If they're smart, they'll juke away from gender roles, human depravity, sexual identity, and racism. Stay away from why you actually need a Savior. Heisman the fact that both pedophilia and lying to your spouse equally distance you from the love of God and that only faith in Jesus can guarantee an eternity with Him.

Basically, they will talk about problems you can work on solving yourself. Talk about how God can help you get out of your present situation or get you through whatever worldly issue is plaguing your life. Oh, and they will make sure to have a dope title for the sermon so the YouTube tagline is on point. If so much of preaching today is focused on improving your life and your circumstances, isn't this just as self-centered and misguided as the classic prosperity gospel? Who is the focus and protagonist of every sermon? I'll help: it's you.

If so much of preaching today is focused on improving your life and your circumstances, isn't this just as self-centered and misguided as the classic prosperity gospel?

If you grew up in the Christian church, your parents and grandparents—including mine—grew up in a time when televangelists ruled the airwaves, specifically the ones who preached the prosperity gospel. The prosperity gospel movement started with traveling revival preachers and miracle healers in the early 1900s, but it has held various forms since then. In her book

Blessed, author and Duke University Divinity School professor Kate Bowler broke down the basis for this teaching of the gospel:

> The prosperity gospel, I argue, centers on four themes: faith, wealth, health, and victory. (1) It conceives of *faith* as an activator, a power that unleashes spiritual forces and turns the spoken word into reality. (2) The movement depicts faith as palpably demonstrated in *wealth* and (3) *health*. It can be measured in both the wallet (one's personal wealth) and in the body (one's personal health), making material reality the measure of the success of immaterial faith. (4) The movement expects faith to be marked by *victory*. Believers trust that culture holds no political, social, or economic impediment to faith, and no circumstance can stop believers from living in total victory here on earth. All four hallmarks emphasize demonstrable results, a faith that may be calculated by the outcome of a successful life, no matter whether they express this belief through what I call "hard prosperity" or "soft prosperity."[2]

From Oral Roberts and Kenneth Copeland to Benny Hinn, Joyce Meyer, and Joel Osteen, for the past seventy years, there have always been larger-than-life religious figures spouting some sort of message that says, "God wants you rich and healthy as long as you put in the work, faith, and money."

It has always flabbergasted me that these people can keep filling churches and even arenas with a message that is so clearly opposite of what Scripture actually says. But maybe it shouldn't. Yes, the Bible uses the words *prosperity* and *abundance*, but not in the same context that many Christians use. God never said that He would just straight up transact with you: you have faith in Him, and in return, you get health and wealth. If we think about it for a second, the logic does not match reality. Let's say God actually does have that perpetual deal for all of us, and we can actually receive material wealth, health, and happiness by having more faith, donating money to a ministry, and really believing that it'll happen. Don't you think if that existed, we would have congregations full of wealthy, healthy, and overall "prosperous" folks? Why are our churches filled with people who are hurting, sick, and struggling financially? Western Christians, just like the rest of the population, are still dying from disease and illness every day and still have just as many financial woes as the next person. Are these congregations filled with people who don't have enough faith or haven't done enough for the kingdom? Are the preachers the only ones who are so anointed that they can receive "the blessings" from God because of their faith? Or maybe, juuuuust maybe, God never promised any of that?

It's pretty easy to identify run-of-the-mill prosperity preachers. They all say things like "Sow a seed" and "Name it, and claim it" or more subtle things like "Don't you think your Father in heaven wants you to be happy?" While they do still have huge audiences, their demographic is steadily growing older and passing away. This leaves a new audience for a totally different type of preacher . . . or are today's preachers that different?

With millennials and Gen Z representing the largest portion of the population of the United States, there is a massive market for a new wave of preacher.[3] And oh boy, have those dudes come out in force. Most of them are, seemingly, based on the Hillsong Church model. If you have taken up residence under your local boulder and have not been paying attention lately, a network of super-fresh dudes with hot wives are leading a new movement of Christianity in pretty much every metropolitan city. Just do a quick Bing search on famous pastors in your favorite city and, guaranteed, a hip-sounding church website will have used their search engine optimization savvy to be at the very top of the results list. That church will probably be led by a guy who looks like he belongs at your local craft-cocktail watering hole instead of a church. But he's there, wearing oversized glasses, megatight jeans, and some Saint Laurent boots or Off-White x Air Jordan 1s.

Guys like Judah Smith in Seattle, Chad Veach and Erwin McManus in LA, Rich Wilkerson Jr. in Miami, Chris Durso in New York City, Robert Madu in Dallas, or the supreme leader of them all, Steven Furtick in Charlotte, North Carolina, not only look good but speak/

perform so much better than the preachers you are used to. They give super-relatable sermons that connect your social media anxieties to the conflict between David and Goliath or that miserable breakup you just went through to the Israelites wandering in the desert. So many of their sermons consist of how God is there to help you get through the challenges of life. And they go heavy on alliteration (hence the title of this chapter), expecting the inevitable "Wowwwww!" from their faithful, front-row fanboys. Rarely, however, will you hear much about the actual gospel in their sermons; the fact that you were born a sinner, are still a sinner, and are condemned to actual hell without the saving grace of Jesus. The hero of the story is usually you, the listener, not the actual Creator of the universe, who put the world into motion.

If you pull away all the delicious rhetoric, mild comedy, and relatable stories, most of the time you will find a heaping dose of feel-good, with very little reference to the words of God.

Look up the transcripts for these guys' sermons. If you pull away all the delicious rhetoric, mild comedy, and relatable stories, most of the time you will find a heaping dose of feel-good, with very little reference to the words of God. This is not the game one should be playing if the goal is to truly lead people spiritually. How many pastors have to be publicly fallen for us to see that we are terrible at living out our personal interpretations of Scripture?

While these guys are seen as hard-core leaders of the faith who are informed directly by the Holy Spirit, they also rarely take equally as staunch, offensive stances on topics that are clearly outlined in the Bible they teach. In 1 Corinthians 1:17–18, Paul spoke precisely to this issue:

> For Christ did not send me to baptize, but to preach the gospel—not with eloquent wisdom, so that the cross of Christ will not be emptied of its effect. For the word of the cross is foolishness to those who are perishing, but it is the power of God to us who are being saved. (CSB)

Basically, Paul was saying that we should never dilute the message of what Jesus did for us on the cross with vague words and emotional rhetoric, because that risks diluting the power of that very act.

In a podcast interview I did with Todd Wagner, founder and pastor of Watermark Community Church in Dallas, Texas, he helped to clearly outline how counter this worldview is to what Jesus actually said in the Bible. Wagner referenced what Jesus said in Luke 12:

> I came to bring fire on the earth, and how I wish it were already set ablaze! But I have a baptism to undergo, and how it consumes me until it is finished! Do you think that I came here to bring peace on the earth? No,

> I tell you, but rather division. From now on, five in one household will be divided: three against two, and two against three. (vv. 49–52 CSB)

So many critics of my account have called it "divisive" and questioned why I would want to "cause so much division." They can't comprehend how anyone could ever question something going on in the modern church, especially when it comes to the Instagram pastors of the world. After all, "they impact more people in a day than you will in an entire lifetime," according to members of the featured churches. It's interesting, though, because according to Luke 12, Jesus clearly encouraged the division of people from one another based on their faith in Him.

I think I understand why the message has become what it is, though. Our attention spans are shorter than ever, and a lot of us want real solutions to the things we are facing right now, not some conceptual thought based on a situation that happened two thousand years ago. Young people have also seen how detrimental previous church leaders have been to those on the fringes of society and are over-indexing on being welcoming, friendly, and focused on love. It also hasn't helped that the majority of voting "evangelicals" elected potentially the most brash and controversial president in history. As a millennial myself, I know that my generation values being authentic, questioning the status quo, and fighting against whatever traditions led to electing such a polarizing president. Since many of our generation's parents and grandparents treated those on the fringe as less than, it seems like it would be easy to grow a congregation with a message of "We welcome everybody and love everybody; Jesus also welcomes you and loves you no matter what. We're attractive and trendy and entertaining, so come on in and stay awhile."

Judah Smith explained it to a journalist from MTV this way:

> I think those of us who believe in God and those of us who follow Jesus, who believe that Jesus is God and the Messiah, I think we have a responsibility. I think it's an honor, but it's a responsibility to carry this differently. The narrative is changing, and we're getting back to actually what Jesus did say and how he lived, which I think is the ultimate in scripture—if we could live, love, and look more like Jesus, no matter what you believe about him, whether or not he's God and savior, the world would be a much better place.[4]

If I had left my parents' church or faith traditions, Smith's rethinking of how to portray Jesus would sure sound attractive to me.

But when does that translate over to life change based on what Jesus actually said and did? When is that leading to meaningful community in which people are open and honest with one another based on biblical wisdom and, as 2 Timothy 3:16–17 says, "teaching, rebuking, correcting and training in righteousness"? What is the long-term road map for making such a welcoming environment? Do any of these churches hit people with the real gospel that says, "Hey, you actually have to address the sin in your life, regardless of how countercultural that is"? Without any of these hard follow-on conversations, this just seems like a new form of prosperity gospel focused on improving our lives and getting what we want on this earth.

Isn't a gospel that says, "You're okay, and God wants the best for you on this earth" and "If you just pray and raise your hands during this hype worship service, you'll be aight" equally as unhelpful as the OG prosperity gospel, just with a better jawline? Isn't this turning the fact that Jesus came to die for our sins and save us from hell into a churched-up version of Tony Robbins's $5,000 seminars?

Again, I understand how we got here. Young people are so sick of stuffy, judgment-laden church services and want nothing to do with them. Of course they will demand and fill the need for services that are relatable and entertaining. Surely, the guys leading these churches mean well and probably want to do good in their communities and in the world (I've spoken with many of them). Is it not worth asking ourselves if this is the correct direction, though? Isn't it worth examining the fruit of these churches—your churches—and asking if the means is producing the desired end? That's all I want you to do: to consider if this is truly what God intended, based on His

Word. I want so much more for the church that I'm a part of and for the faith that I proclaim to believe. I want that for you as well, to not waste time on earthly pursuits via entertainment and distractions but to focus on the One who can actually save us from the sin that plagues us all.

Discussion Questions

1. What are some things that contemporary churches do well to reach people for Christ?
2. To reach the culture for Jesus, at what point do we go so far that we actually leave the Bible's truths out of the message?
3. How do we balance being attractional versus encouraging repentance?

Chapter Nine

SIX FLAGS OVER JESUS

Where Does Production Value Stop and Vanity Start?

One of my best friends in the world, Benjamin Samuel Adams, asked if the "Six Flags over Jesus" chapter was going to be the sixth chapter in my book. I'm purposely making this the ninth, just so his obnoxious pun doesn't hold water.

In Louisiana, when I was a tyke, my idea of a megachurch was the one with the tallest steeple. If you're like me, you still have no idea what the point of those are. According to Jack Wellman, "The bells called us to worship, the steeple told us where worship was, and the verticality of the churches directed our attention upward toward God as we entered the church for worship services and may have originated in Europe."[1] Okay, well, that answers that.

As a junior high kid, I thought that a megachurch was the one with the most TVs, the best gym, and the most babes at youth group meetings. I couldn't imagine more than five hundred people showing up for church on a Sunday. I thought each church's worth and size were measured via the amenities. Megachurches were there to host your birthday parties or a Power Team performance or *Halo* tournaments, not to raise hundreds of millions of dollars and operate a complex pseudocorporation and real estate holding firm. Now things are a little different.

The great country of Texas is known for a lot of big things (everything's bigger in Texas, right?). We have massive sports franchises, filthy-rich oil and gas tycoons, exquisite barbecue, stable economies, miserable heat, and, of course, behemoth megachurches. Just *yuge*! Some of the biggest churches in the country, in terms of attendance, reside in Texas. The easy target is Joel Osteen's Lakewood Church in Houston, which touts a weekly, live, in-person attendance of more than fifty thousand people (and one large rotating globe).[2] The only way to fit this many people was to literally buy the former Houston Rockets arena for $7.5 million back in 2010.[3] Then there's Gateway Church, which started in Southlake (basically Dallas) and now attracts more than one hundred thousand people a week at multiple campuses.[4] And let's not forget Prestonwood Baptist Church, which boasts forty-six thousand people across three campuses per week,[5] and Fellowship Church in Dallas, which attracts more than twenty-four thousand people a week.[6] This is only four within a four-hour drive, and only the ones with more than twenty thousand people showing up for the weekly worship sesh.

The term *megachurch* commonly refers to "Protestant congregations with weekly worship attendance of 2,000 or more adults and children."[7] While there is a formal definition, it's pretty common knowledge within Christian circles that megachurches have several nonnegotiables to be considered "thriving," "contemporary," or "hip."

Obviously, you need a huge band led by a Ray LaMontagne impersonator and supported by a babesauce secondary vocalist and pseudochoir that can—almost—sway in unison. The band should be playing on $10,000 Taylor acoustic guitars with pedalboards chock-full of $250 effects pedals and complete with $4,000 Nord keyboards. The singers need $400 Shure SM7B microphones and $1,200 64 Audio in-ear monitors. The stage will also need a full spread of LED wash lights and moving headlights, lasers (tasteful ones, obv), and maybe a couple of skating rink–era smoke machines. On top of that, you'll need at least three massive projection screens with HD projectors and an eighty-inch LED TV on which the pastor can project his sermon points. You will also need a dining table–sized soundboard, light board, and video board, in addition to the racks of speakers that could have easily been taken from an Electric Daisy Carnival show.

In the lobby you will most definitely need a fully functioning coffee shop with coffee brought back from the most recent missions trip, an indoor jungle gym, a bookstore (filled with the pastor's books for sale), and plenty of seating with free Wi-Fi and Pottery Barn–style lounge chairs. Everything needs to look and feel more like a Starbucks Reserve in Chelsea Corner than a church lobby. This will be the setup of the main campus, which

Everything needs to look and feel more like a Starbucks Reserve in Chelsea Corner than a church lobby.

will then project the "experience" to a more church-lite version via satellite campuses.

It sounds like I'm being extreme about the gear and amenities involved with these places, but I guarantee that if you walked into any church advertised to have two thousand attendees or more a week, you'd find a variation of this type of setup. As a member of a megachurch in Dallas, I can personally attest to taking advantage of these amenities.

I took a poll from my Instagram tribe asking about the craziest thing they have seen in a megachurch, and these were some of the responses:

"Northland Church has a Nature's Table [basically a Tropical Smoothie] Cafe in the lobby."[8]

"Willow Creek in Chicago has an arcade, food court, cafe, and two waterfalls."[9]

"Inspiring Body of Christ Church has a literal aquarium with exotic fish and a post worship dive show every Sunday."[10]

Are you starting to see the dollar signs add up? While there are exceptions, many of the churches with this slew of amenities identify as "seeker sensitive" or holding to the "attractional model" of church. This direction toward super-comfy buildings and services started in the '80s and mirrored the business models and entrepreneurial spirit of the decade. My friend Kate Bowler wrote about this in her book *Blessed*:

> Some theorists predicted that these baby boomers were spiritual wanderers whose comfort in big box establishments—university classrooms, corporate cubicles, and Walmart aisles—predisposed them to church models that resembled these large institutional forms. . . . Church growth strategists hoped to capitalize on this by making contemporary churchgoing feel as comfortable as trips to the mall. Continuing in this commercial vein, experts recommended that churches implement marketing strategies and view their church as a product and their worshippers as consumers.[11]

And that's the rub: the church experience has turned into the equivalent of a leisurely trip to the mall, a place where you can fulfill all of your soul's desires. It makes sense that these methods improved with the progression of technology and media, further resembling the entertainment establishments of the time.

Now, this is a pretty standard formula if you're building a campus in the South or Midwest, but the new trend on the coasts is to set up camp in a vintage (maybe haunted) theater or school in the epicenter of a

The church experience has turned into the equivalent of a leisurely trip to the mall, a place where you can fulfill all of your soul's desires.

metropolitan city. There will be young, beautiful people outside waving big signs reminiscent of those shopping center insurance places, taking breaks to record a new Boomerang to post on the church's social feeds. The coffee will be an upgrade as well, Blue Bottle or Philz if you're lucky. The theater will have to be primo real estate because of the convenience and attraction factor; maybe some druggies or sex workers will stumble in off the street at 10:00 a.m. on a Sunday after a night of various activities. ZOE Church, Mosaic, Hillsong NYC, and VOUS Church all subscribe to this model in some way, another part of their super-attractive Instagram motif that young people love.

Now back to Texas: Prestonwood Baptist Church, which in Dallas is affectionately referred to as "Six Flags over Jesus," is the source for the name of this chapter. This massive compound of 140 acres in Plano, Texas (voted best place to live in 2019 for people with student loan debt, for some reason),[12] is famous for its sprawling campus and yearly Christmas pageant that attracts attendees from all over the country. Selling thousands of tickets, Prestonwood brings in a slew of live animals, fills the show with every type of Vegas-style show talent imaginable, and has even had . . . wait for it . . . levitating neon drummer boys.[13] This spectacle can only be compared to the year-round exhibition that is the campus itself. The buildings include a pre-kindergarten-through-grade-12 school, a café, and a fitness center with outdoor sports fields. In 2008, the church expanded to include a second campus of 127 acres in Prosper, and in 2017, Prestonwood launched an Español campus in Lewisville.[14]

Prestonwood has achieved massive scale and is able to use that scale to help serve the community. The church even has a crisis pregnancy center that has served more than seventy thousand people with pregnancy tests, ultrasounds, consultations, classes, and assistance.[15] Hard to argue with that. Is this wide-scale community impact a result of the enormity of the campus, though? Is it based on the size of the church buildings and the production of the Christmas program? Does all of the production start to feel like too much? Is it even worth asking if there is a better way to do church?

Another example closer to Fort Worth is Gateway Church in Southlake, led by Pastor Robert Morris, where Christian music superstar Kari Jobe once led worship while on staff. This place is almost as gargantuan as Prestonwood. A *Fort Worth Star-Telegram* article from 2017 stated the following:

> The church reported revenues of $127.2 million in 2016. Gateway's expenses totaled $123.9 million, $3.5

> million less than total revenue, according to its annual report.
>
> Gateway spent $9.9 million on land and other expenditures in 2016, which includes the land for the Frisco location and the Dallas campus.
>
> The megachurch boasts $218.7 million in assets.[16]

The vastness of these numbers is hard for me to even fathom for an organization whose core mission is to go and make disciples. Hopefully the majority of those dollar amounts are going to that mission.

While Judah Smith and his wife, Chelsea, pastors of Churchome in LA and Seattle, have appeared on my account for their extensive Gucci collection, Judah has made some pretty impactful statements and contributions to the overall church ecosystem. One thing I heard him say on the *RELEVANT Podcast* was, "What if we could spend thousands and reach millions rather than spending millions to reach thousands?"[17] He was referencing his Churchome app and the newfound success it had in the wake of the extensive social distancing caused by the coronavirus pandemic.

Many church leaders and laypeople (myself included) wrote him off for trying to re-create a church environment online . . . oh, how the turntables, though. COVID-19 forced all of us to shelter in place, and the majority of megachurches had to bring church online. And Judah? Well, he was just posted up laughing his way to the proverbial bank (or maybe the real bank; I'm not sure). Anyway, his point was basically made for him because this single season of sheltering in place caused the gospel and/or church experience to be more scalable in the digital environment than ever before. Millions of people were tuning in to different churches across the globe that they never had access to before. The cost? Most likely millions less than the capital expenditures for the expansive campuses built in your nearest city.

I get why these places were built; it makes sense that in a season of attendance growth and membership, a church feels the need to continue building out a space to accommodate all those people. But at what cost? Sure, some of these churches are able to impact the community. At what point, though, are we willing to say as believers in Jesus that all our production, equipment, amenities, and commerce have become gluttonous or vain? Where does production excellence stop and vanity start? I totally get the argument that if God has gifted us with talents and abilities, we should use those for His glory in the most excellent way possible and to reduce distractions from Him. That could include using lights and sound in an excellent way. But when is it too much? Can it be too much? This is a macro level of the same discussion of whether or not it's okay for preachers to wear expensive sneakers. At a certain point, does the overdone production serve to elevate the entity, the building, or the organization and detract from the attention we need to be paying to God?

I am absolutely not against large church buildings. Buildings in and of themselves are inanimate objects and have no morals, heart, or spirit. I even get why churches feel the need to erect impressive structures and spaces that appeal to mass gatherings or draw people in. I do question the benefit being worth the cost, though.

Where does production excellence stop and vanity start?

It's interesting to think about how we got to this point of massive church campuses when that was rarely, if ever, modeled in the Bible. Sure, in the Old Testament there was a Jewish temple in Jerusalem, and there were synagogues in the New Testament, but the Bible offers no instructions or guidance on the modern-day, weekly production that we are used to. In his article for *RELEVANT* magazine, John Pavlovitz provided a pretty convincing counter to the current understanding of what "church" is supposed to be:

> The early believers were essentially in-house churches, where immediate family, extended family and friends were already living in deep, meaningful community together. They didn't have to rent out space and a sound system and start service planning.
>
> They were already living life together organically and so they didn't need to create a destination to foster community. These groups absorbed the new converts,

> but there is no evidence of the healthy evolution of these communities into organized churches. The only mention we have is in the book of Revelation, where large, opulent churches are being chastised for their corruption and apathy.[18]

Clearly God doesn't care about the size, scope, or paint color of our church buildings. He cares about His people, how they commune together in His presence, and their heart toward possessions. Pavlovitz put it this way:

> Jesus never promises that with size or organization . . . there would be more of His presence. He didn't leave building instructions or establish an organizational structure or provide liturgical templates. He affirmed that his people and his presence were the only necessary ingredients. They would come to the table together, and He would take a seat there with them. Your kitchen table, a bar in a tap-room, a bench at the park, a coffee shop. He is present there.[19]

Practically speaking, depending on the church, there is probably merit in constructing a useful and maybe even beautiful home base. Who would ever want to stop a "healthy" church from growing to a certain size and being able to accommodate that growth? Defining church health is an issue in and of itself, though, because as my friend JP says, "Cancer grows rapidly too." If your church

If your church is seen as "healthy" just by the speed and amount of growth, you may be missing out on some key elements.

is seen as "healthy" just by the speed and amount of growth, you may be missing out on some key elements.

Let's say that your church is healthy and growing; then of course you would need to care for the people attending your church services. That includes providing a space for them to come, meet, and encourage one another. But in his book *Healthy Church by Design*, Timothy Songster cautioned against dependence on the building: "Spiritual renewal won't happen by acquiring a permanent building. It will happen through prayer and proclamation of the Word of God."[20]

My older brother, Matthew, is an extremely eloquent writer and thinker. Being an actual enlisted combat veteran Marine and having a master's of philosophy from Biola University, he's the one out of our family who actually deserves to be a published author. He's also super-ripped, which is unbearably frustrating. My whole life has turned out to be one big attempt at one-upping him; I became a Marine officer, and I will forever rub this book in his face (probably won't beat him in the abs department, though). Regardless, he runs a wordy-yet-compelling blog (probably the only one remaining on the internet) called *Coffilosophy*, where he pens shortish essays about various heady topics. After a trip to Europe, he wrote a piece about the Vatican that more artfully describes the same questions I have about the church's obsession with buildings and amenities:

> For what was all this made? Was it that man might revere God, or that he might submit himself to the glory of Rome? Were such exorbitant commissions weighed solemnly against the plight of the starving? Or were Rome's marbled halls too thick to admit of their cries? . . . Does God look upon such extravagance in the name of "the Church" with favor or with contempt?
>
> I thought that what had begun as the Body of Christ had become captive to a host of ghoulish intruders: humility had been bound and gagged, and on her throne sat a loathsome successor: Power.[21]

Again, I don't have a problem with church buildings/campuses in a vacuum; they clearly serve a purpose and are the product of immense giving and membership growth. I purely want to examine if this model is the best way to do church. Is our concept of church in the Western world the ultimate form of worship and service to God? Can we improve this at all? Do our coffee shops, jungle gyms, fitness centers, and bookstores equal a more divine experience with our Creator or an increased number of salvations? Has our desire to perform the most "excellent" service and production slowly transitioned into being a vain practice to cater to human desires? Maybe this is the best way to do it. Maybe the huge bands, massive real estate holdings, and Christmas productions are the divinely inspired way to gather. Maybe I'm the only one who's got questions, but I at least want to encourage you to wrestle with this too.

Discussion Questions

1. What has been your criteria for choosing a church and/or switching churches?
2. To you, where does production value stop and vanity start?
3. Other than a weekly service, what are some of the tangible impacts that your church has produced?

Chapter Ten

CHURCH MERCH

What Happens When a Harmless Brand Becomes Our Golden Calf?

If you grew up in the '90s, you probably remember the wave of "Jesus juke" T-shirts that hit the market in line with the "throw away all your Bone Thugs-N-Harmony CDs" movement. Back when brick-and-mortar retail was a thing, if you went into any Christian bookstore—or Southern truck stop—you would see a vibrant display of branded tees that, from far away, looked recognizable but close up were a little . . . off. Mildly tacky adaptations of your favorite graphic swag, like "A breadcrumb and fish" in the style of Abercrombie & Fitch, "got Jesus?" resemblant of the "got milk?" advertisements of old, or a bright-orange tee with "Jesus, sweet Savior" on the front that looked an awful lot like the Reese's logo. You may have even owned similar items back in the day. No judgment here, since as you know by now, I was homeschooled, so you'd better believe I was decked out in imitation cultural swag. I think this must've been my parents' attempt at assuaging my desire to be cool and, dare I say, relevant while also continuing to shelter me from the big, evil cultural monsters emanating from MTV and Comedy Central. Basically, homeschool parental judo. *Tip of the cap*

From my perspective, Western Christian culture loves to accept pop culture just enough to sloppily morph it into their own. I'm not sure if it's an attempt to be "in the world, not of the world" or if it's a protest altogether, but either way, it's kinda cringe. It's not just T-shirts either; you can get pretty much any product out there, save an Xbox (I checked) with Jeremiah 29:11 on it.

From my perspective, Western Christian culture loves to accept pop culture just enough to sloppily morph it into their own.

Fast-forward to nowish, and there is a new trend that puts a modern spin on the goofy Christian bookstore garb of the '90s: church merch. If you want to start a church to reach young people, you need not only a nondenominational, action verb–sounding name, like *elevation*, *transformation*, *action*, *potential*, *impact*, and so on; you also need some dope abstract branding. Hopefully, with your slick naming convention and beautiful influencer team, you can attract young graphic designers who will make a mysterious yet memorable logo for your new church at a (*Borat voice*) great price. Maybe you'll even hire them onto your creative team for $30,000 a year—it's for the kingdom, ya know? Once you get a sick logo, you can now create an entire streetwear brand and merchandise the heck out of it.

Some of the heavy hitters in Instagram church—can we just call it that already?—have some pretty extensive apparel lines. The dudes Rich Wilkerson Jr. at VOUS Church and Chad Veach at ZOE Church have full web stores where they sell everything from socks and hats to shoulder bags and sweat suits. For the VOUS Conference in 2019, the church even made a T-shirt with all of the speakers' faces—their faces—on it, like a mix between a tour shirt and a wolf tee.[1] In the spring of 2020, VOUS made Easter-themed coronavirus quarantine masks, which are no longer available, and tees; they have since deleted the posts.[2]

"How interesting that you're commenting about churches creating streetwear brands," says the reader. "Don't you literally sell PreachersNSneakers hoodies and tees as well?"

Is there a difference between an idiot on Instagram selling merch to stay afloat and a religious group developing a brand and subsequent retail strategy instead of pointing to the One they're supposed to be all about? It's a short leap to think people buy this stuff so they can be seen as associating with the group. That's literally why people buy my merch. Does it matter if it's a church selling these items? This is something I am constantly grappling with.

Brands, in and of themselves, are amoral; selling merchandise is amoral, as long as that merchandise was produced in an ethical way. As people in the Western world, most of us are either consciously or at least subconsciously obsessed with brands. For the average person, you probably desire some brand that promises to improve your life. Maybe it's Nike or Lululemon, which promises to make you an elite athlete or a ripped Instagram model. Or maybe it's YETI coolers and their promise to make you a better fisherman or frat star all while keeping your one small bag of ice frozen for a week.

The purpose of a brand and a brand identity, according to Will Kenton at Investopedia, is to "distinguish their product from others. . . . Companies [or churches, for the sake of our argument] become very closely associated with . . . , if not synonymous with, their brand. The more the brand is worth, the higher brand equity it is said to have. . . . The company is often referred to by its brand, and they become one and the same."[3]

Philosophically, what happens when a church establishes itself as a brand? Hasn't it now developed an identity focused on distinguishing itself from others? I wonder if a deeper discussion is needed about the convergence of brands and Christianity. I wonder if these can appropriately exist and intersect at the same time. I wonder if my friends Joshua and Ryan at the Minimalists have the right idea trying to minimize the power that brands have over our lives.

I have zero problems with the concepts of branding, commerce, or capitalism. I'm literally writing this book during the final months of my master's of business program at Southern Methodist University (SMU) and got my undergraduate degree in marketing from the University of Arkansas. (Go Hawgs.) The thing about capitalism, though, is that it makes churches change their focus from serving the poor and broken to promoting profit and ownership.

The thing about capitalism, though, is that it makes churches change their focus from serving the poor and broken to promoting profit and ownership.

Churches, unlike any other organization, are charged with leading people to the Creator of the universe and making disciples out of those people—an immense calling. But as individual Christians, we are called to do the same. If you're creating an additional brand out of your church or even yourself, thereby elevating the people and aesthetics of that organization or person, are you detracting from the One who actually deserves the attention, reverence, and glory? Are you also generating a sense of exclusivity between those in your church and those outside of it? Have we just written this form of branding and consumerism off as a natural progression in modernizing evangelism? Or is it worth asking if there is a better way?

Everyone's favorite new evangelical, Kanye West, really brought this concept into the mainstream with the creation of Sunday Service, specifically his performances at Coachella in 2019. This was the first time Kanye and his massive choir performed for the public. They built a mountain out of dirt and sod just for the performance and entered wearing some culty-feeling, matching red garments. In true Kanye fashion, the entire thing was weird and shocking and also impossible to ignore.

One parallel story line that came from the performance was the Sunday Service merch table. Most of us are used to band merch tables with slightly overpriced tees; we pay the price to commemorate the experience. Kanye's merch was, uh, way pricier. Like $50 pairs of socks that said "Jesus Walks" or "Church Socks" and $225 crewneck sweatshirts that said "Holy Spirit" on the front and "Sunday Service at the Mountain" on the back. In my opinion, this was the most public display of connecting "church," streetwear, and secular music. After that, seemingly every megachurch in the country was on board with developing merch that had streetwear elements. "If Kanye is doing it, then the kids must love it. Let's do our own."

From the outside looking in, *GQ* writer Sam Schube penned an article about the optics of this phenomenon, saying that this new trend of church merch and the entrance of the "hypepriest" (a term he coined) reflect a lot of the things that are discouraging about the fashion world.[4] We are always being marketed to and made to focus on exclusivity and scarcity. One of the big elements surrounding streetwear is how limited or unique the pieces are, which drives up demand. Generally, streetwear brands will do "limited runs" of their apparel to drive up hype and, hopefully, the willingness to pay.

In the context of church or faith, what's the purpose of leveraging those elements? Maybe if the leadership of a church sees doing so as an opportunity to draw new, impressionable kids into the fold, it has a strategic purpose. Schube responded to that thinking, specifically regarding ZOE Church's merch, saying, "I don't know that it's a *bad* thing . . . if they feel that that's the most effective way to draw the sort of young, city-dwelling crowd that they want to attract, more power to them. If you're joining a church for the t-shirt, it better be [cool]."[5]

My friend Whitney Bauck also wrote about the players in the church merch game in a 2017 article on Fashionista:

> Zoe Church isn't alone in occupying this space. Other megachurches all over the country have debuted similarly street-appropriate merch in the past few years. Montana- and Utah-based Fresh Life Church has "Snakebird" shirts inspired by Jesus' command to his disciples that they be "wise as serpents and innocent as doves." The youth ministry of Christ Tabernacle Church in New York has "Misfit"-branded sweats and denim that allude to the way that Christians are encouraged to see themselves as "in the world but not of it."[6]

Wilkerson's VOUS Church is on the forefront of the merch game.

For its 2015 conference, the church tapped Fear of God designer (and outspoken Christian) Jerry Lorenzo to design its T-shirts. As with any hot streetwear drop, some of those pieces found their way to resale sites like Grailed, where they sold for as much as $190. It's worth noting that this was before Bieber's own collaboration with Lorenzo on his Purpose tour merch ignited a flurry of sales amongst Beliebers and jawnz enthusiasts alike.[7]

The convergence of actual fashion designers and IG churches is here to stay and only seems to be growing in popularity. A handful of companies online cater solely to fulfilling church merchandise requests. There is a product market fit and money to be made.

If these churches are using merch as an attraction tool, is it worth questioning the motive or nah? If you're bringing people in because of the T-shirt, are you really being authentic in what you're selling? I don't know; it's probably fine.

There's a story in the beginning of the Bible that seems relevant to this. In the book of Exodus, Moses literally received the Ten Commandments from God on Mount Sinai, and the Israelites were waiting for him to come back down. Chapter 32 describes God's people growing impatient:

> When the people saw that Moses was so long in coming down from the mountain, they gathered around Aaron

> and said, "Come, make us gods who will go before us. As for this fellow Moses who brought us up out of Egypt, we don't know what has happened to him."
>
> Aaron answered them, "Take off the gold earrings that your wives, your sons and your daughters are wearing, and bring them to me." So all the people took off their earrings and brought them to Aaron. He took what they handed him and made it into an idol cast in the shape of a calf, fashioning it with a tool. Then they said, "These are your gods, Israel, who brought you up out of Egypt."
>
> When Aaron saw this, he built an altar in front of the calf and announced, "Tomorrow there will be a festival to the LORD." (vv. 1–5)

God saw this and told Moses to go down the mountain and straighten up the Israelites.

> "They have been quick to turn away from what I commanded them and have made themselves an idol cast in the shape of a calf. They have bowed down to it and sacrificed to it and have said, 'These are your gods, Israel, who brought you up out of Egypt.'" (v. 8)

The long and short of it is that Moses was able to ask God to spare these people, but Moses melted the golden calf, ground it into powder, scattered it in the water, and made the Israelites drink it. Yikes!

Oh, yeah, and after that, God "struck the people with a plague because of what they did with the calf Aaron had made" (v. 35). In the words of the prophet DJ Khaled, "Congratulations, you played yourself." God does not play about His people building idols to try to replace Him. Not doing this is literally in the Ten Commandments: "You shall have no other gods before me" (Ex. 20:3).

Okay. Relax, bro. There's a huge difference between constructing a gold statue of a cow to replace God and a couple Fear of God–style hoodies.

Is there? Are both scenarios not constructing something as an object of elevation, though? Just think about it for a second. Church merch brands are literally there to highlight the cool vibes and attractiveness of that specific church and the people involved with it. To some, this may make it seem like one church is better than another. At a minimum, people are using interesting-looking pieces of clothing to rep their church body. At most, they're distinguishing themselves from the pack in a way that makes the organization, not God, seem elevated over the rest.

Church merch brands are literally there to highlight the cool vibes and attractiveness of that specific church and the people involved with it.

Again, I realize that I, too, have sold merch in the past. I'm probably selling it as you're reading this book. This isn't a discussion about capitalism in general—that needs another book in itself—this is a discussion about its place in the church. I'm one dude running an Instagram account; I am not a church, nor do I claim to be or want to be one. I understand that it may be difficult to distinguish what I do online versus what the church does.

PreachersNSneakers, a media and retail entity, probably looks a lot like what the Western church does every day. These systems being conflated, which makes them difficult to distinguish, is the very thing I'm asking about. Does the fact that churches resemble retail stores compromise the thing that's supposed to be set apart? Since both retail stores and churches have cash registers and web stores, do you get why it's hard to see the difference between the two? Even if you think I'm a hypocrite and shouldn't be selling merch, then what does that say about what many churches are doing? If it's inherently problematic that a guy says one thing but does the other, what's your take on the church doing the same thing? Again, you may be offended that I would even ask the question about whether the church's effectiveness has been limited by this move to retail-and-profit focus, but I would challenge you to look inward and ask yourself why.

It very well might not be appropriate for any of us to sell branded swag, but then again, most of us don't have a dedicated group of congregants donating to fund our lifestyle (*ducks*).

Discussion Questions

1. How do you feel about churches creating brands/merch? Is it not that big of a deal?
2. Do you think brands in general detract from pointing to Jesus?
3. How should religious institutions balance their retail strategy with their outreach strategy?

Chapter Eleven

CALLOUT CULTURE, CHRISTIAN TWITTER, AND CLOWNING PASTORS

When Can Christians Question Public Figures from Afar?

Knowing I was raised as a Christian homeschooler (maybe that's redundant), you can probably guess the type of lifestyle my siblings and I lived; the stereotypes around homeschool kids exist for a reason. School dances were especially traumatizing. Most of our days were spent muscling through boring workbooks; reading wordy, classical literature; or working on our chosen musical instruments. Initially, we all had to learn piano, but thankfully, after my extended griping, my parents let me transition to playing the drums, the ultimate chick magnet (or so I thought).

In our Louisiana town, the homeschool community was pretty small but tried to interact together in hopes of salvaging the immense social deficit that came with doing our learning at the homeplace. We went to museums, local plays, and skating rinks together (we made sure they didn't play any Spice Girls so as not to fully corrupt our impressionable Christian souls). We shared activities and experiences as well as convictions and beliefs.

One of the strongest beliefs in our community was that we needed to distance ourselves from mainstream culture, hence the desire to school at home. In an effort to be "in the world, not of the world," the homeschool and broader Christian community in our town participated in several nationwide boycotts against pop culture icons. In 1997, the Southern Baptist Convention officially announced that it was boycotting the Disney corporation due to its support of the LGBTQ+ community.[1] The homeschool collective in our town followed suit, and we, the children, had to grapple with the fact that we would never get to experience Disney World and all of its sweaty, overpriced glory.

While we can debate for days about whether the SBC's boycott of all things Disney was wise or effective, as I look back, this was the first time I participated—even if passively—in what I now understand as "cancel culture." After the Disney boycotts, I also participated in the Metallica CD smashing and MTV-avoiding practices that were commonplace in the '90s and early 2000s in the Southern church world. Cancel culture and its lesser form, callout culture, has been around a long time, but it's now more lethal to lives, careers, and reputations than ever before.

Cancel culture and its lesser form, callout culture, has been around a long time, but it's now more lethal to lives, careers, and reputations than ever before.

For those of you who like to maintain your mental health and not delve into the relentless cesspool that is Twitter, "cancel culture," "callout culture," or "online shaming" is, as Jonathan Merritt put it, "a term for what happens when people, most often on social media but increasingly in 'real life,' band together and employ shaming tactics to block a person from having a platform. It can mean boycotting the target's businesses, refusing to consume their books or films or pressuring friends, colleagues and activists to denounce them or formally cut ties."[2] If you don't spend much time on Twitter, you can do a quick search online to find myriad examples of public figures, brands, and celebrities being dog-piled on for something they did, said, or didn't say or do.

One of the most prominent examples in recent years has been the "me too." Movement, where men and women all across the world used Twitter and other social media platforms to publicly denounce and share their own experiences of sexual abuse, assault, and harassment, oftentimes getting the accused fired, jailed, or just pressured to explain themselves—usually for good reason. This is precisely what happened to famed Hollywood mogul Harvey Weinstein when he was accused of sexual assault by a slew of actresses over his decades-long career. A major contributing factor to his arrest and conviction was quite literally people leveraging callout culture to bring awareness to what he had done. This instance was absolutely a net positive, as Weinstein was eventually found guilty for his years and years of crimes.

In the modern-day Christian social media world,

this type of campaign exists, and it doesn't look much different—maybe a few less cusswords, but the premise is still there. Often it happens for good reason, and other times it seems misdirected. We as Christians can be just as relentless with one another as the next guy.

Take famed "canceled" hipster pastor Rob Bell, for instance. In youth group, we devoured every bit of content this guy would put out. His *NOOMA* videos admittedly led us to some great small-group discussions and gave our youth pastor, John O., a break from having to come up with relevant talking points. The times were tacky, so it was refreshing to experience some biblical truths that had a Jony Ive–Apple vibe instead of a whole wheel's worth of cheese, like most church content of the day.

Years after we had fully bought into Rob Bell's theological swag, he wrote and published a book called *Love Wins*, which basically questioned the existence of hell and our understanding of the term. Obviously, this did not go down well with many Christian leaders who espoused strictly biblical interpretations of heaven and hell. Pastor John Piper, who is known for being unabashed about adherence to Scripture and the inerrancy of it, famously tweeted, "Farewell Rob Bell."[3] And so commenced Bell being canceled by much of Christian culture. Rob Bell has parlayed the canceling into more of a mainstream career, however, and seems to be doing just fine for himself, appearing with Oprah and being named among the top one hundred most influential people by *Time* magazine.[4]

Lauren Daigle was also the target of the Christian cancel mob. The wildly popular vocalist, who evokes serious Adele vibes, was eviscerated online after she chose to perform on *The Ellen DeGeneres Show*. Ya know, the one that most normal people trying to build a music career would jump at the opportunity to perform on. Because Ellen is openly gay, the conservative Christian community took this as Lauren bowing to societal pressure and not standing up for biblical values.

In a later interview about the performance and backlash, Lauren said, "In a sense, I have too many people that I love that they are homosexual. I don't know. I actually had a conversation with someone last night about it. I can't say one way or the other. I'm not God."[5] Many Christian leaders and talking heads did not love that answer, thinking that she should have been bolder or more direct about her views on homosexuality. While Lauren went on to continue crushing it in both secular and Christian markets, she did feel the immense heat that can come when you don't appease the cultural majority you represent.

On Christian Twitter, there are loads of tweets and comments about abusive church leaders or organizations mismanaging money or politicians who butcher the Christian faith or preachers who are seen as heretics or false prophets. Everyone gets the opportunity to say their (often) uninformed piece about how someone should or shouldn't be acting or preaching or whatever. You can burn hours of time reading through rants and critiques about the state of the church or how Trump sucks or how the Popeyes chicken sandwich is better than Chick-fil-A's. All could be valid takes, founded in research and complete emotional neutrality . . . but they rarely are.

Kate Shellnutt wrote an outstanding article for *Christianity Today* about this very topic. I wish I could paste the whole thing here because she freaking nailed it:

> The bar for what merits a public reckoning has fallen as the internet incentivizes us to speak up, call out, and shout down. . . .
>
> Being on the receiving end of a barrage of negative feedback can ruin your day, your year, or your career. Any defense, explanation, or apology could rile up further condemnation. This critical attitude dampens our dialogue and betrays a cynical attitude toward our digital brothers and sisters.[6]

She went on to say that while it may seem unloving or ungracious to attack Christians online, this behavior is an inevitable by-product of our collective experience of years and years of bad actors receiving overwhelming benefits of the doubt. After all, how many examples of deception, abuse, or embezzlement must we experience before feeling compelled to call them out online? But then at what point have we swung too far in the opposite direction?

And therein lies the problem with callout culture: everyone—literally everyone—gets to inject their opinion into something they may know nothing about or have an immense bias toward. There are numerous examples about a person, brand, or company getting dog-piled over something that was taken out of context, misquoted, or even just completely false. The power of social media at the scale of hundreds of millions of people can yield devastating results. The accused or "called out" can lose their jobs in minutes; their reputations destroyed, they may even fear for their lives.

Therein lies the problem with callout culture: everyone—literally everyone—gets to inject their opinion into something they may know nothing about or have an immense bias toward.

Why would we ever want to inflict this on someone? Especially as Christians, shouldn't we, as Kate said, "hope for the best and forgive one another quickly when others inevitably fall short"?[7] I think so. But aren't there also some things worthy of screaming about at the top of our lungs to whoever will listen? What about racial injustice? What about abuse of power? What about sexual assault? Are you okay with someone highlighting those things? Do you care what happens to the person being accused of such heinous crimes? What about the more nuanced takes that you believe strongly about? Issues like women serving as pastors in your church or members of the LGBTQ+ community being affirmed in their Christian faith or protecting the lives of unborn babies: Is callout culture appropriate when used in defense of these topics? If someone is violating or threatening what you believe to be a resolute fact, shouldn't you use every platform necessary to get the word out?

This is the tension we need to sit in: When should we use our platforms to enact justice, and when should we display grace and humility? I honestly don't know, but I bet the answer starts with seeking wisdom from Scripture and wise counsel.

What about the issue of gossip? Critics of my account have equated PreachersNSneakers to a forum for gossip and "unwholesome talk," saying that I should mind my own business. According to Got Questions, the Hebrew word for *gossip* means "one who reveals secrets, one who goes about as a talebearer or scandal-monger."[8] Pretty strong words. Basically, anyone who reveals privileged information that isn't theirs to tell or tells false stories about someone is gossiping. Intent also plays a role: "Gossipers often have the goal of building themselves up by making others look bad and exalting themselves as some kind of repositories of knowledge."[9] Online, these are called "clout

Critics of my account have equated PreachersNSneakers to a forum for gossip and "unwholesome talk," saying that I should mind my own business.

chasers," basically those who seek notoriety or attention by bringing others down.

On the surface, this sounds exactly like what I'm doing by pointing to shoe price tags. It absolutely would be if I were intending to bring these dudes down or dismantle Christianity.

What if in my deepest convictions I saw the church being misrepresented or mischaracterized? Am I to stay silent then, even if someone's feelings might be hurt? These are public figures representing the church of Jesus who have said, "Look at me; follow me; hear what I have to say." If you choose to put something out into the public domain, it is no longer privileged information. My intent was never to bring anybody down, and I stand by that. If you think I'm malicious after reading this far into the book, then I'll never be able to convince you otherwise. But objectively speaking, if communicating facts is amoral, then is my spreading the facts about how much these shoes are worth still gossip?

I agree that gossip is hurtful, but what about criticism or critique of things that a person has chosen to publicly post or portray? Gossip absolutely happens within the PreachersNSneakers comment section, but not universally. What ownership or accountability do I hold for creating that environment? I struggle with this because the logic forces us to drill down to the ideas of social media, celebrities, and our public lives as a whole. If my account is gossip, then any other account that spreads news about public figures is also gossip. Anytime you talk about what Kanye or Bieber or the Kardashians are up to, that's gossip. Have you wrestled with that? Can we actively participate in social media at all and also not be gossiping?

There are plenty of verses in the Bible about not spreading false witness or talking bad about someone. James wrote about not speaking evil against one another and how powerful words can impact someone's life (James 3; 4:11–12). Proverbs emphatically declares that gossip will separate friends, and perverse people stir up conflict (16:28). In the book of Romans, gossips and slanderers are listed among other types of terrible sinners who receive God's wrath (1:29–32).[10] In that same list, though, are nouns like *greed* and *envy*, as well as descriptors such as *arrogant*, *boastful*, and *insolent*, some of the characteristics of famed megachurch pastors who represent our faith and have publicly fallen.

If you had a hunch that your pastor was exhibiting some of these characteristics, wouldn't you at least raise a proverbial flag and address that? Would you feel compelled to say something? I guess that's why I struggle with the idea that my account is gossip. Yes, I see the negative comments, and yes, I see the inferences you could make about my intentions, but that's not my heart. Some would argue that I'm disingenuous, pretentious, and adhering to a double standard or that I hate the pastors I'm featuring on PnS. But if you believe that what I'm doing is driving a meaningful conversation, then how could it be gossip? What if it's actually tough love toward the church, saying we all need to take an inventory of what we value, promote, and elevate? Is our church being honest about where our treasures are?

We Christians have a pretty solid gauge for measuring whether our content and/or commentary is worthy of a follower of Jesus. In Galatians 5, Paul said:

> You, my brothers and sisters, were called to be free. But do not use your freedom to indulge the flesh; rather, serve one another humbly in love. For the entire law is fulfilled in keeping this one command: "Love your neighbor as yourself." If you bite and devour each other, watch out or you will be destroyed by each other.
>
> So I say, walk by the Spirit, and you will not gratify the desires of the flesh. For the flesh desires what is contrary to the Spirit, and the Spirit what is contrary to the flesh. (vv. 13–17)

Paul then described a whole list of desires of the flesh and basically said that anyone who lives out those desires will not inherit the kingdom of God:

> But the fruit of the Spirit is love, joy, peace, forbearance, kindness, goodness, faithfulness, gentleness and self-control. Against such things there is no law. Those who belong to Christ Jesus have crucified the flesh with

> its passions and desires. Since we live by the Spirit, let us keep in step with the Spirit. Let us not become conceited, provoking and envying each other. (vv. 22–26)

It's pretty hard to argue with that if you say you believe and follow the Bible.

The tough part about writing this chapter—well, really this entire book—is that it could be self-indicting. It *is* self-indicting. The reason you are reading this book right now is because I was able to put a spotlight on the issues—or, at least, perceived issues—of pastors, preachers, and worship leaders flaunting flashy garb for all to see. Quite literally, I was subtly and humorously calling out leaders of the faith to wrestle with the fact that their clothing is worth more than the typical congregant's monthly mortgage payment. I achieved this using social media; creating an attractive platform to show what I thought seemed to be a strange cultural issue that needs to be addressed.

The tough part about writing this chapter—well, really this entire book—is that it could be self-indicting. It *is* self-indicting.

Before I created the account, I was a nobody and had zero intention of causing a stir. My actions were purely meant as a joke, a way to process my own annoyance via social media. If I were to go back and do it all over again knowing what I know now, I would obviously do some things differently. But I still believe that sparking a global conversation that caused people, both believers and non, to reevaluate for themselves what they expect of their faith leaders and their own public and private personas, has been a worthwhile pursuit, even if there has been messy collateral damage. I don't want anyone to get harassed or berated or abused—ever. I'm not sure how to prevent that, though, given how many terrible people there are on the internet and how everyone has equal access to comment. As a regular person who is not a public figure and has no platform of any kind, how do I cause a stir or effect change without taking the risk of putting something controversial out into the public? Had I known how to do that effectively and with perfect Christian grace, I would have done it that way.

I did a whole host of things wrong with the PreachersNSneakers account. At the very beginning, I projected motive onto a whole group of dudes I knew nothing about. I had a literal minute of inspiration to make some comments about how expensive their shoes were and just assumed that only my friends would see my content. I had never had anything go viral before, so why expect this to? Even so, after it did go viral, I bought into the massive growth and energy that started to surround my account and realized that it had turned into something much bigger than I ever intended, both positive and negative. I continued to post even though I didn't know what my plan or intent was, because I had so many voices around me saying that what I was doing was so righteous and helpful.

I originally assumed that the people I featured were getting money from the offering plate and funding their lifestyles with it. I had no idea that people gifted pastors with new kicks or cars or houses. I also never intended to do this from behind the veil of anonymity. My original posts weren't anonymous; there was no reason for them to be. With my limited (read: zero) amount of experience with going viral or having a huge platform, I tried my best to make decisions that were as wise as possible—namely, to stay anonymous until I had a grasp on what I wanted to do with my newfound "fame." I quickly started to see people getting heated about the topic, and I didn't know what else to do to protect my family and press onward in the right way. In the eyes of many, this was seen as cowardice. People constantly objected to what I was doing and said things like, "How is it that you are trying to hold others accountable without allowing yourself to be accountable as well?" My first response to that was that I never intended to "hold anyone accountable"; I just saw something I thought was ridiculous and wanted to make some ill-informed comments about it. But I see why people would say that.

I'm confident that I'm not a coward but wish I had come out in public immediately so I could be above reproach in that regard. To this day, I'm still not sure if the method I used to bring attention to all this was the best choice. When I see followers being terrible to one another in the comment section, I question if that's the healthiest form of generating discussion. Many think it's not, but many others think it's immensely effective, which causes me to ask again: When is an issue big enough to denounce or highlight publicly? And when is it okay to circumvent 1 Corinthians 6, which basically says Christians should settle disputes among one another instead of in the secular public realm, and make sure something is addressed immediately? What about the "me too." Movement or the countless public-figure pastors who were discovered to be abusing their power? Are we to sit back and hope that the wrongdoers' close communities will do something about their actions?

The bottom line is this: people started questioning the status quo of the church and the lifestyle of famous preachers after my account came to light. There is no denying that. There is also no denying that some people's feelings got hurt throughout it all, and I feel deep remorse for that. Again, had I known what I know now, I would have considered going about the account in a different way—or at least having a more defined strategy moving forward.

The bottom line is this: people started questioning the status quo of the church and the lifestyle of famous preachers after my account came to light.

Many of my critics have also brought up Matthew 18:15–17

as a reference that speaks exactly opposite to the methods I was using to call out Christian leaders:

> If your brother or sister sins, go and point out their fault, just between the two of you. If they listen to you, you have won them over. But if they will not listen, take one or two others along, so that "every matter may be established by the testimony of two or three witnesses." If they still refuse to listen, tell it to the church; and if they refuse to listen even to the church, treat them as you would a pagan or a tax collector.

The issue I have with using this reference with regard to what I was doing on Instagram is that I honestly did not know if preachers wearing expensive sneakers was a sin or not. I still don't. Nothing in the Bible talks about clothing requirements for leaders of the faith. Deep down the apparel felt icky to me, but I didn't know why. If I was immediately convinced that these guys and girls were sinning, then yes, absolutely I should have gone to them in private first to get their side of the story. At the time, however, I didn't feel strongly enough to actually reach out to any of these preachers, because it didn't seem like a huge deal. It just seemed like something worth commenting on to my immediate group of friends.

I am confident that had I reached out to Steven Furtick, with his three million Instagram followers, and said, "Hey, bro, each week you have on a new designer outfit that's worth thousands of dollars. Do you see why that would mess with some people?" my message would have gotten ignored, deleted, or—*maybe*—answered with boilerplate language by an assistant.

This whole conversation begs a bigger question about those Christians who choose to be public figures: Do we still owe them the Matthew 18 treatment of going to them in private if they've chosen to put their whole lives on display? If you sign up for the benefits, followers, and influence of being a massive public figure, should those followers still admonish, question, or encourage you privately? How is this supposed to work? There isn't much in the Bible about the topic of how to address sin with people whose lives are on display for all to see, and I still struggle with what to do. Are we supposed to just trust that these guys have a circle of advisers who are holding them accountable? Is their local church body holding them accountable? Many megachurches are led by single families and don't even have elders. Even if they do have all that, if we perceive sin in the church leaders' lives and see it affecting the message of the gospel, are we to stay silent? What if we do reach out for a one-on-one conversation and we get crickets? Can we then use a larger platform to call out sin? I'm just not sure.

I wonder if the discomfort of this whole conversation stems from years and years of Christians being hush-hush about money. For some reason, most of us grew up treating money as a private issue. I felt the same. Who are you to say what I can and can't do with my money? Who are you to judge me for what I do when you have a bunch of jacked-up stuff in your own life? Surely this has something to do with why we have been averse to pointing out this stuff in the past. If we call out others about their use of money, it pretty much instantly makes us feel like hypocrites. How often have you used money frivolously or spent it on something you purely wanted and didn't need? That's the tough part about this whole thing, and it still makes me squirm today and feel like I'm not minding my own business.

I wonder if the discomfort of this whole conversation stems from years and years of Christians being hush-hush about money.

But how many Christian leaders, media moguls, and public figures have operated for years sexually assaulting employees, embezzling funds, and swindling people out of their hard-earned money for personal gain? What if your grandparents were among those whose money was stolen by Pastor Kirbyjon Caldwell? The Houston megachurch pastor pleaded guilty in 2020 to defrauding investors of millions of dollars, money that went to his personal cars, mortgages, and vacation properties.[11] Would you care about hurting feelings then? Would you care about minding your own business? The only reason those guys were found out was because someone, somewhere was courageous enough not to mind their own business.

Kate Shellnutt ended her *Christianity Today* article this way:

> The body of Christ is directed to live out the call to "believe all things" and be "wise as serpents," to be a model of loving, truth-seeking community—even online. But we will not restore trust by shouting at or shaming the voices who push back or rush to judgment. We will only do it by offering a steady, faithful witness over time—living our lives and filling our feeds in a way that proves that we can be trusted.[12]

I agree. The only way we can be seen as a source of meaningful commentary, wisdom, or direction is if we consistently display the fruit of the Spirit in our daily lives. If we feel a pull to advocate for something or to fight against injustice or fraud or false teaching or whatever, it would behoove us to seek wise counsel, biblical insight, and prayer before launching into an online tirade or callout campaign. There is no denying that there have been positive outcomes from callout culture, but the outcomes have been met with their fair share of messy social media shrapnel, which can quickly turn to vitriolic fodder for the keyboard warrior. I firmly believe that some issues are worth screaming about from the top of our lungs using every platform we have. We must weigh the facts, context, and risks associated with opening that proverbial can of worms, though, and accept the potential consequences. Choosing when and how to do that will always be a perpetually complex and imperfect challenge.

Discussion Questions

1. When do you think it's okay to call someone out online?
2. What are other examples of positive outcomes of callout culture?
3. How do you think we should address public figures? Should we at all?

Chapter Twelve

WOW! YOU READ TILL THE END

What Do We Do Now?

It's interesting how a trivial thing like the price of sneakers can cause such a global stir, generating philosophical discussions about the ethics of making money from preaching, the existence of Christian celebrities, or whether God actually uses a Gucci belt to bless you. At the same time, I had no idea that a Christian debate could be attractive to mainstream celebrities and those who are just fans of streetwear. Movie stars, musicians, and social media influencers all jumped on the hype train that I created from my phone while sitting on my couch in Dallas. The idea that one of my favorite drummers ever, Questlove, would wear one of my hoodies for a red-carpet premiere still blows my mind. I had the opportunity to talk with John Mayer, Hayley Williams from Paramore, and Zach Lind from Jimmy Eat World all because I put the value of a shoe next to a preacher wearing that shoe. The world seemed to care infinitely more about these issues than I ever could have forecast.

The list of people who publicly wore my merch is something I'll never understand: Adam Devine, Joel McHale, Lena Waithe, Trey Kennedy, Luke Cook,

Nathaniel Buzolic, Abner and Amanda Ramirez, Jacques Slade, Andy Mineo, Marty Santiago, Brian Foster, Chris McClarney, Aaron Chewning, Wordsplayed, Matt Wertz, and others. I still don't quite know how to live in the tension of doing something people think is funny or thought-provoking without buying into thinking that I'm awesome or talented or gifted somehow. I absolutely don't want to be a celebrity or famous or whatever, but I do want as many people as possible to grow in discernment, understanding, and reverence of the Christian church today.

Through a whole host of factors and circumstances, the impact of our faith has been shrouded by all of the noise created by our attempts to look like the world or to dismantle it. Spending the last four years with an immensely controversial president who aligns with "evangelicals" has made it easy to clown the church as a whole. The gaudy church buildings, worship productions, and larger-than-life celebrity leaders have reduced the appearance of Jesus to just another form of weekend entertainment that resembles a pyramid scheme where the people at the top collect the spoils and the commoners at the bottom continue to spin their wheels, hoping for more. We have allowed our churches to become inadvertent temples to fashion, production, and comfort, all in the name of relatability and being approachable. We are using churches as political campaign stops to further a partisan agenda that is antithetical to the way Jesus lived—whether it be Right or Left—and there doesn't seem to be any sign of stopping, as our country sprints toward further division. Congregations of these megachurches continue to fill with people who want a check in the box, an answer to their guilt but no real desire to grow deeper in their pursuit of God.

Up to this point, public questions about pastors' lifestyles have been relegated to only the top five richest guys, as we make fun of their private jets and quaint mansions. There is general consensus about that being ridiculous, but now (I hope) more Christians are willing to ask about the new market of faith leaders and the benefits of their ministries versus the risks. Namely, whether the hype-priests and prosperity pastors of today are just furthering the Christian entertainment marketplace, starving the need for actual biblical teaching and in the meantime lining their pockets and building up their platforms and influence.

While there has been constant debate in the comment section and in the media about the efficacy and appropriateness of my approach, there is no denying that it got people talking, thinking, and (hopefully) laughing. The PreachersNSneakers account allowed Christians and non to point to something that they had long felt was off within the Christian community (celebs included). The idea that you could get rich from being a pastor, preacher, or worship leader did not sit well with many, but I didn't really know why at first. PreachersNSneakers forced me and others to wrestle with why we felt what we felt. It forced pastors to wrestle with the fact that some of this critique might be valid or worth considering. A podcast listener emailed me recently about the idea of questioning the money aspects of faith, saying, "It is just refreshing to know I can wrestle with these thoughts, too, and still love Jesus." That's what I truly want for everybody: the grace to wrestle with doubts and questions that may have made you feel guilty in the past. God's not scared of your doubts, questions, or concerns. He hears you, sees you, and wants to spend eternity with you, as hard as that is to comprehend.

That's what I truly want for everybody: the grace to wrestle with doubts and questions that may have made you feel guilty in the past.

The idea of prosperity has been at the forefront of these discussions around for-profit faith and wannabe celebrities. It's very easy to write off the traditional prosperity gospel as a manipulative ideology that just benefits the one spouting it. It's also easy for someone like me to fall into an overly cynical view of the world and God. If I'm honest, I often see God as one who doesn't care about any of our worldly needs or logically has bigger fish to fry. I struggle to see why God would place me in such a fortunate position to have air-conditioning, Wi-Fi, and grocery delivery while billions of people barely live on two dollars a day.

You would think that He would be more focused on those who are fighting for their lives than the ones fighting for a promotion. There are many days when I believe God would never care to actively bless us with material, social, or financial gain in order to make us happy or joyful or whatever. It seems to be putting God in such a small box to say, "Please, God, help me find a parking spot at this mall" or "Jesus, please help this presentation go well" or whatever the equivalent is for you.

Now you, correctly, should be saying, *Whoa, dude, that's a miserable way to view a God who says He loves you.* I'm just trying to keep it real with y'all. We may never understand why a select few get to live in the West with relatively good health, wealth, and objective success while others starve or get malaria or some other miserable death sentence that they did nothing to deserve. We may never understand why even some people in America get incurable cancer or lose their best friend or go to prison as an innocent person, and we get to chill on Instagram, wishing for more stuff or more vacations. I don't know why or how this can be the way God designed life to be.

Having studied this idea of prosperity for the last year or so, I've come to the conclusion that God—in His incomprehensible wisdom—does wish for us to flourish even though other people suffer. I absolutely don't understand that. My friend Stephen Graves calls this the "radical middle," where we don't live expectant for God to give us tons of money, but we also pray for blessing and good health for those we love who have a need. I can't deny his point that wealthy people have used their fortunes to improve the world. In his book *Flourishing* he wrote:

> I've reframed the "Prosperity Gospel" as the *Shalom* Gospel. I believe God is a good God and desires us to flourish. He blesses each of us with experience and opportunity that He expects to be used for His glory and honor. He wants us to utilize prosperous circumstances in order that we might bring blessing to all. We are to seek peace and wholeness for ourselves and for others. When we do that, when we seek prosperity in our own contexts, we are living out a dynamic and whole gospel.[1]

With our limited understanding of God and His character, this seems to be where we need to live while also having grace for ourselves to not have to explain every confusing or unfair scenario about the state of the world. While I believe that God does want us to flourish, I also believe that we don't approach God and ask Him for the things He is truly capable of. Sure, I'll ask for wisdom, healing, or peace, but will I ask Him to dissolve homelessness, save entire countries, or radically change even the most evil of people? Do I ask God for the things that sound insane to even think of? Do I actually believe that He can do more than just give us our trinkets and 3 percent cost-of-living raises?

I really don't care about who wears which sneakers or how much they cost. I do care about how our faith is being represented to the world. The people we choose to idolize in our strange Christian subculture—those who are actually talented and not just notable on Instagram, like your boy—are the ones the world sees as our representatives. I want to continuously push those who have been blessed with immense talent and influence to elevate the name of Jesus and make their own names less. This is an imperfect struggle that we all need to continuously strive for, myself included.

I really don't care about who wears which sneakers or how much they cost. I do care about how our faith is being represented to the world.

Hopefully this book has caused you not only to ask hard questions of yourself and of your faith leaders but also to take action. I hope after reading this that within your faith community you can be armed with meaningful questions that allow you to further protect yourself and your leaders from the allure of fame, power, and money. I hope you can take the opportunity to go back over your social media feeds and audit why you posted what you did while also considering how your friends may see it, knowing that you might have to delete a super-fresh vacation pic or not post about your new whip. I've had to do the same, cringe captions and all. I hope you reflect on who you view as celebrities and ask how much time and energy you devote to following them versus how much time you devote to God. I hope you grow in discernment to keep your local church leaders accountable as well as encourage them in the relentlessly difficult job of pastoring others. I hope you continue to challenge the status quo and not rest in how things have always been or seem to be heading.

If you're like me, you probably want some defined action steps. While the whole premise of this book is to sit in the tension of not having all the answers, I think there are some realistic things we can do, focused on giving, serving, and listening. The bottom line is that we can all do better when it comes to serving others and not gratifying ourselves. While many of the questions I have raised don't have super-defined answers (yet), I believe that we can actively push toward a more humble and generous posture, constantly emulating Jesus' lifestyle.

While many of the questions I have raised don't have super-defined answers (yet), I believe that we can actively push toward a more humble and generous posture, constantly emulating Jesus' lifestyle.

Going back to the book *Rich Christians in an Age of Hunger*, author Ron Sider provided a helpful list of guidelines for giving if you find that you are too consumed with stuff and status. I know it's helped me. The list is paraphrased below:

1. Pursue a lifestyle that could be maintained over a long period of time if it were shared by the entire world.
2. Fight against the urge to confuse luxuries with necessities.
3. Examine your reasons for spending/buying and whether or not they are legitimate.
4. Maintain suspicion of your desire to buy into fads. Pursuing hobbies is one thing, but be wary of your desire to jump all-in on the latest craze.
5. Fight to understand the difference between the "occasional celebration" and "day-to-day indulgence." (My wife and I struggle with this because we're always looking for a reason to eat more Blue Bell ice cream.)
6. Understand that the amount you earn doesn't equally dictate what you buy. Basically, don't buy stuff just because you can.
7. Find a balance between short-term, immediate-relief giving versus giving to fix long-term structural issues (e.g., giving to support hurricane relief compared to giving to improve the long-term viability of a people group).
8. Give not only to missionaries and churches but also to orgs that are meeting basic human needs.[2]

Another helpful study of wealth and giving comes from the book *God and Money* by Gregory Baumer and John Cortines. The authors broke down two categories into seven total principles.

The first category is wealth, and it breaks down into the following principles:

1. All things we think we own actually belong to God.
2. Our wealth should be used for serving His kingdom.
3. Wealth has great potential for both good and harm.
4. Worldly wealth is fleeting, and only heavenly treasures are eternal.

The second category is giving:

1. Giving generously to those in need is a moral duty in a fallen world.
2. Giving should be voluntary, generous, cheerful, and needs-based.
3. Giving generously releases us from the grip that money has on us.[3]

If you expect others to be doing more for the poor, widow, and orphan, you'd better be doing it too. In addition to it being the right thing to do, I have found that by-products of serving are that things and people don't "own" me, as well as a renewed sense of joy and fulfillment in life. Here are some practical things you can do to serve those around you that will hopefully help you let go of the stuff and status you hold:

1. If you don't already serve in some capacity, contact your church and ask how you can serve this week. Don't deliberate on it; don't overthink it; just freaking do it.
2. Contact those close to you, ask how they're doing, and offer to bring food, help them move, mow the lawn, or something else. Don't think about or expect anything in return. We should all have a posture of wanting to serve our people without looking for an ROI.
3. Knock on your neighbors' door, introduce yourself, and try to get to know them. You would be surprised how life-giving this can be, even if it's awk at first.

Not only do we have work to do in our own lives, but we should also strive for clarity, honesty, and accountability from our faith leaders. If you're involved in a local church, here are some things we should all be doing:

1. If you have questions about your faith leaders' lifestyles, you should—wait for it—ask them about

it. If it's messing with you like it did me, consult your community about your concerns, then reach out to that person or staff. It's fair to ask those living off support from the local church about their spending, and it just might be the thing that keeps them from succumbing to temptation. At the same time, be prepared to account for your own finances as well.

2. Ask for clarity from your church regarding finances. If you are unsure about how your church is deploying your tithes overall, you should ask.
3. As my friend JP put it, we should all try to "kill the hero," which means to fight against elevating anybody within the church except for Jesus.[4] We should be very careful when we generate hype around any person or thing that is not Jesus.

Social media, Christianity, and money are an extremely sensitive and potentially dangerous combination. None of us really have it figured out. Everyone has equal access to you and the life you choose to present online. Everyone gets to judge you based on what you post and what you do. As Christians, we must not only figure out how to be decent online but also try to figure out how to emulate Jesus' lifestyle in a world that looks a lot different from His time on earth.

According to Paul Tripp, we should all be questioning and analyzing our time spent on social media:

> Now, because of the power of social media, anybody can become an authoritative voice, can begin to speak to critically important issues without ever having gone through those normal institutional accountable ways of garnering authority. And I would just ask you the question, "Who are the authoritative voices in your life and how do you know those voices are trustworthy?" . . .
>
> This tool [of social media] that is enormously beneficial for good is also a powerful tool of sin and temptation, and we need to be honest about that. The church is being weakened by that, by the fact that we are now comfortable with exposing ourselves to things that we should have never exposed ourselves to. . . .
>
> What is your talk like on social media? How helpful is it to others? How much of it is motivated by love and grace and joy and patience and faithfulness and mercy?[5]

The bottom line about money is this: our hearts are what matters. Going back to the book *God and Money*, Cortines and Baumer's conclusion about money and its place in the life of Christians is incredibly concise: "It is not poverty in itself that makes one blessed by God, but the humble, dependent, God-trusting disposition that we often find accompanying the oppressed poor in Scripture. Likewise, riches themselves are not wicked, but only if they are unrighteously obtained or used, a condition that is found only too frequently in this fallen world."[6]

I'm very grateful for the opportunity to help people grow deeper in their faith or at least ask hard questions in pursuit of a more authentic faith and spiritual walk. I don't count myself as more anointed or gifted or talented; I don't know why God made (or allowed) this whole thing to happen or why He made me the point person for this discussion. But I truly believe that He had a hand in it, and I'm honored that I might be able to be used by Him in a minuscule way to help others find Him or develop a renewed respect for Him and His glory. I do plan on asking about this period of life when I get to heaven and trying to understand why He chose to work in such mysterious colorways.

ACKNOWLEDGMENTS

I don't deserve this book, this platform, or this attention. I don't know why this happened or why God chose me (or allowed me) to be the guy to bring up all these questions. Only once in my life have I ever watched YouTube worship videos in lieu of going to church, and only once in my life have I felt so compelled to show the world how much clergy footwear is worth. From the outside, I'm sure many of you can't understand why people care so much about the lifestyles of pastors, but for some reason, many do. As a card-carrying idiot who has doused himself in mistakes and who perpetually removes the foot from his mouth, I am grateful for the opportunity and recognize that a whole host of people helped me—dragged me—along the way.

To my wife, Stacy, who has not only followed me across the country to ultra-luxurious Marine Corps bases but also stuck with me as I pursued miserable jobs, failed entrepreneurial endeavors, years of full-time school, and a messy viral social media experience—all with a smile on her face—you are the closest thing to the prosperity gospel that I have ever experienced. You have provided wisdom that has saved me from embarrassment and shame more times than I can count. I love you more and more each day and hope that I can sell more than twenty books so I can give you the same freedom to dream and experience life that you gifted me. I don't deserve you but am so grateful that I get to live life with a babesauce angel woman that I could not have even dreamed of. You are so lucky to have me.

To my parents, thank you for the love and support through all my misguided phases of life and for providing a safe, loving home for me in a world that can be so cruel and unforgiving. You were the first display of gospel grace in my life, and I am forever grateful. Please continue to give me a heads-up before y'all visit, though . . .

To my brother, Matthew, and sister, Catherine, and their spouses, Whitney and Rich, thank you for enabling my twisted sense of bitter humor and for always backing me up when I needed it most. I'm #blessed to have you all in my life.

To Seth Jones for encouraging me to create Preachers NSneakers and for giving me my first bump of publicity. This is all literally your fault, so thanks . . . I guess?

To Mack Brock for unknowingly causing a global stir by wearing some borrowed Yeezy 750s in a YouTube video. I'm eternally grateful.

To my media manager, Shelby Massey, thank you for all the hours and mental health you saved me by managing the ever-entertaining comment section and DMs of my account.

To my agent and literary crutch, Jonathan Merritt, thank you for taking the chance on and believing in the message of this book. I would not have a book without your guidance, straight talk, and willingness to put up with my complaining. While a large percentage of my royalties are going to you either way, I'll thank you to be polite.

To Damon Reiss, Beth Adams, Kyle Olund, and the rest of the W publishing team, thank you for believing in this book and for giving me the opportunity to share it with the world.

To Joel and Sarah McHale for generously opening their home to Stacy and me. Joel, thank you for the hours of time and advice in my writing pursuits, including writing the foreword to this literary masterpiece. I hope to one day have an exclusive sponsorship deal with Pepsi and Laffy Taffy just like you.

To Adam C. Gil for basically creating my logo for free and my first run of merch.

To Ben Nye for being the most consistent friend throughout my entire adult life. I would never help you move the amount you have helped me move.

To John O'Leary for hazing me spiritually in high school and helping me develop a foundation of studying the Bible, memorizing scripture, and not being scared to stand up and communicate my faith.

To Justin and Shekinah Holiday for not only gifting us our first real pairs of sneakers but also being such committed/generous friends to our family.

To Zane Callister for all the free help you gave starting my podcast. Everyone's ears thank you as well.

To Jonathan Pokluda for selflessly giving me advice throughout this whole thing and providing a great example of living out a biblically informed life while also trying to fight against the notoriety that comes with writing and speaking.

To Todd Wagner for leading our church with wisdom, courage, and devotion to teaching from the Bible.

To John Mayer for following my account and for your smooth, silky tone. You'll prob never see this, but it's fine.

To Questlove for wearing a PnS hoodie to the *Shaft* world premiere.

To the rest of the Kirby and Berry family, thank you for the laughs, support, and food that both directly and indirectly influenced this book.

To my ride-or-die friends (in no particular order): Justus and Stephanie Murimi, Kade and Claire McDonald, Zach and Melanie Binns, Jason and Rachel Delph, Rose and Dave Delph, Ben and Lydia Adams, Rawles and Laura Bell, Nick and Addie Hauser, Daniel Dodd, Phil and Kayleigh Crabtree, Nick and Rachel Pavey, Parker and Erin McCormack, Nelson and Natalie Fleming, Scott and Taylor Bradshaw, Phillip Smith, Kirby Colvin, Daniel Steed, Brooks and AnnaChristen Scoggin, Tommy and Alli Russell, Greg and Krisi Barnes, Michael Walker, Nathan and Claire Gertson, Lori Watkins, Meagan Williamson Lee, Colby Warren, John and Kelli Claybrook, Will and Natalie Bostian, Jonathan and Christine Kaskow, Will and Anna Richardson, Wesley Clingman, Halley Burnett, Emily Vanderstraaten, Bryan Gammon, Holly Carpenter, Corben and Jamie Young, Ken and Regina Young, Michael Yantzi, Hunter Ward, Joseph Allen, Max Fanning, Jake Mott, Chris Hembree, Spencer and Katherine Blevins,

Scott and Katie McFadin, Alex Seikaly and the rest of the SMU MBA Class of 2020, Dave and Garrah Welk, Hudson and Jessie Smith, Natalie and John Cox, Tonya Zunigha, William Nix, Alnoor Dhanani, and others I've definitely forgotten, thank you for being true friends throughout my life and supporting me when much of the internet did not.

To all my new Instagram friends: Annie F. Downs, Sarah Spain, Katelyn Tarver and David Blaise, Karin Kildow, Luke and Aimee Rodgers, Chris McClarney, Tony Hale, Marty Santiago, Taylor Johnson, Erica Greve, TK McKamy, Luke Cook and Kara Wilson, Jacques Slade, KB, Wordsplayed, Matt Wertz, Dave Barnes, Carlos Whittaker, Ronny Chieng, Caitlin Parker, Emma Crist, Aaron Chewning, Audrey Assad, Travis Greene, Luke Barnett, Tanner Thomason, Abner and Amanda Ramirez, Justin Stuart, Adam Busby, Joshua Fields Millburn and Ryan Nicodemus of The Minimalists, Tim Chan, Jamie Tworkowski, Kate Bowler, Beleaf, Jake Triplett, Trey Kennedy, Knox McCoy, Kristina Hart, Johnny Giovati, Jaron Myers, Brian W. Foster, Ryan Mullins, Manuel and Anjelah Johnson-Reyes, Jake and Rachel Scott, David Nasser, Kat Allen and Katelyn Fletcher from KlearCut Media, Yeezy Busta, Aaron Gillespie, and probably forty others that I can't recall right now . . . thank you for inviting me into your world and treating me like an equal.

To my exes, congratulations, you slept.

To the hundreds of companies that turned me down for real jobs while I was writing this book, enjoy those super cool cubicles and 3 percent raises. I'm sure it's totally worth it.

NOTES

Chapter 1: That Time I Blew Up the Internet

1. Sam Schube, "Hypepriests: The Grail-Wearing Pastors Who Dress Like Justin Bieber," *GQ*, August 7, 2017, https://www.gq.com/story/hypepriests-pastors-who-dress-like-justin-bieber.
2. C. S. Lewis, *Mere Christianity* (Westwood, NJ: Barbour, 1952), 102.
3. Eve Poole, *Buying God: Consumerism and Theology* (New York: Church Publishing Incorporated, 2019), 69.

Chapter 2: Harley Moments

1. Brandon Showalter, "James MacDonald Used Church Funds for African Safari, Lavish Vacations, Says Former Staff," *Christian Post*, March 12, 2019, https://www.christianpost.com/news/james-macdonald-used-church-funds-for-african-safari-lavish-vacations-says-former-staff.html.
2. MacDonald was compensated $1.24 million in 2015, $1.37 million in 2016, $1.387 million in 2017, an unspecified amount in 2018, and $1.27 million in 2019, plus bonuses. See Sally Wagenmaker, *Harvest Bible Chapel—Legal Evaluation Report* (Chicago: Wagenmaker & Oberly, 2019), 3, https://www.harvestbiblechapel.org/wp-content/uploads/2019/11/Report.HBC_.Legal-Eval.with-Forensic-Accounting.2019-11-21.pdf.

3. Wagenmaker, *Harvest Bible Chapel—Legal Evaluation Report*, 7.
4. James Connery et al., *Count Us In: Seattle/King County Point-in-Time Count of Persons Experiencing Homelessness, 2019* (Seattle: All Home/ASR, 2019), 7, http://allhomekc.org/wp-content/uploads/2019/05/2019-Report_KingCounty_FINAL.pdf.
5. Sutton Turner, "Sutton Turner Memo Recommended Raise for Driscoll for FY2013 to 650K Salary, Retain 200K Housing Allowance for CY2013," *WenatcheeTheHatchet* (blog), October 20, 2014, http://wenatcheethehatchet.blogspot.com/2014/10/sutton-turner-memo-recommended-raise.html.
6. Ruth Moon, "Acts 29 Removes Mars Hill, Asks Mark Driscoll to Step Down and Seek Help," *Christianity Today*, August 8, 2014, https://www.christianitytoday.com/news/2014/august/acts-29-removes-mars-hill-asks-mark-driscoll-matt-chandler.html.
7. News division, "Mark Driscoll Peddling Signed Copies of His Sermon Notes," Pulpit and Pen, July 8, 2019, https://pulpitandpen.org/2019/07/08/mark-driscoll-peddling-signed-copies-of-his-sermon-notes/.
8. Relevant staff, "What Is Going with John Gray's Church and Ron Carpenter's $6.25 Million 'Retirement' Package?," *Relevant*, February 12, 2020, https://relevantmagazine.com/god/what-is-going-with-john-grays-church-and-ron-carpenters-6-25-million-retirement-package/.
9. "Feuding Mega-Churches Redemption, Relentless File Competing Lawsuits in Greenville County," WYFF News 4, updated February 7, 2020, https://www.wyff4.com/article/feuding-mega-churches-redemption-relentless-file-competing-lawsuits-in-greenville-county-pastors/30814830.
10. Ryan Nelson, "Beat the 80/20 Rule and Level Up Giving at Your Church," Pushpay, July 5, 2019, https://pushpay.com/blog/80–20-rule-church-giving/.

11. Jacobellis v. Ohio, 173 Ohio St. 22, 179 N. E. 2d 777 (1964), https://caselaw.findlaw.com/us-supreme-court/378/184.html.

Chapter 3: Kanye, Kim, and Carl

1. Marshall McLuhan, *Understanding Media: The Extensions of Man* (United Kingdom: McGraw-Hill, 1964), title of chapter 1.
2. Caleb Parke, "At Passion 2020, College Students Raise over $1.2M for This Cause," Fox News, January 3, 2020, https://www.foxnews.com/faith-values/passion-2020-college-bible-christian.
3. "Mosaic Conference 2019 FAQ's," Mosaic, https://mosaic.org/CONFERENCE-FAQs.
4. "100 Million Mastermind Experience: The Most Epic Gathering of Elite Entrepreneurs Ever Assembled,"100 Million Mastermind, http://www.100mme.com/media/.
5. Ruth Graham, "The Rise and Fall of Carl Lentz, the Celebrity Pastor of Hillsong Church," *New York Times*, December 5, 2020, https://www.nytimes.com/2020/12/05/us/carl-lentz-hillsong-pastor.html.
6. "Pastor Carl Lentz $plurges, but Not Like Other Pastors," TMZ, April 16, 2019, https://www.tmz.com/2019/04/16/carl-lentz-defends-splurging-expensive-shoes-pastors/.
7. Alex Shultz, "Kanye West Asked His Employees to Not Have Premarital Sex," *GQ*, October 24, 2019, https://www.gq.com/story/kanye-west-premarital-sex-no.
8. Ellie Woodward, "Kanye West Told Kim Kardashian That Her 'Sexiness Hurts His Soul' in an Argument About Her Met Gala Dress," BuzzFeed News, updated October 16, 2019, https://www.buzzfeed.com/elliewoodward/kim-kardashian-kanye-west-argument-met-gala-dress-too-sexy.
9. Christi Carras, "Kanye West Praises the Lord—and Himself—at Joel Osteen's Megachurch," *Los Angeles*

Times, November 18, 2019, https://www.latimes.com/entertainment-arts/music/story/2019-11-18/kanye-west-joel-osteen-service-lakewood-church.

10. Janelle Griffith, "Chance the Rapper Is Documenting What He Calls His Religious 'Sabbatical' to Study the Bible," NBC News, December 12, 2018, https://www.nbcnews.com/news/nbcblk/chance-rapper-documenting-what-he-calls-his-religious-sabbatical-study-n947291.
11. Tara Isabella Burton, "Hillsong: The Evangelical Megachurch That Helped Save Justin Bieber's Soul—and Image," Vox, October 1, 2018, https://www.vox.com/identities/2018/10/1/17596502/justin-bieber-hillsong-carl-lentz-married.
12. Lisa Capretto, "Why Justin Bieber Was Baptized in an NBA Player's Bathtub," HuffPost, October 14, 2016, https://www.huffpost.com/entry/carl-lentz-justin-bieber-baptism_n_57fec80fe4b05eff55817389.
13. Rob Haskell, "Justin and Hailey Bieber Open Up About Their Passionate, Not-Always-Easy but Absolutely All-In Romance," *Vogue*, February 7, 2019, https://www.vogue.com/article/justin-bieber-hailey-bieber-cover-interview.
14. Justin Bieber, "Yummy," *Changes*, copyright Universal Music Publishing Group, 2020.
15. Sam Schube, "Hypepriests: The Grail-Wearing Pastors Who Dress Like Justin Bieber," *GQ*, August 7, 2017, https://www.gq.com/story/hypepriests-pastors-who-dress-like-justin-bieber.

Chapter 4: Bad and Boujee? More Like God and Gucci!

1. Kate Bowler, interview by Brian Lamb, "Q&A with Kate Bowler," C-SPAN, February 5, 2018, https://www.cspan.org/video/transcript/?id=56967.
2. Jonathan Merritt, *Learning to Speak God From Scratch* (New York: Convergent Books, 2018), 154.

3. Merritt, 154.
4. Carol Kuruvilla, "North Carolina Pastor Says Swanky $1.7 Million Mansion Is a 'Gift from God,'" *New York Daily News*, October 30, 2013, https://www.nydailynews.com/news/national/north-carolina-pastor-1-7-million-home-gift-god-article-1.1501934.
5. Mike Todd (@iammiketodd), "It's Sunday Morning!" Instagram, July 5, 2020, https://www.instagram.com/tv/CCQ6tbfh9kq/.
6. Steven Furtick, "No One Can Stop God from Blessing You (Except You)," YouTube, June 15, 2018 (from February 15, 2018, sermon "Embracing Limitations," Elevation Church, Charlotte, NC), https://www.youtube.com/watch?v=QNgTqDtLXnU.
7. UNICEF and World Health Organization, *Progress on Drinking Water and Sanitation: 2015 Update and MDG Assessment* (Geneva: WHO Press, 2015), 4, cited in "Global Water, Sanitation & Hygiene (WASH): AssessingAccess to Water & Sanitation," Centers for Disease Control and Prevention, last reviewed June 22, 2017, https://www.cdc.gov/healthywater/global/assessing.html.
8. "U.S. and World Population Clock," United States Census Bureau, September 28, 2020, https://www.census.gov/popclock/.
9. Ronald J. Sider, *Rich Christians in an Age of Hunger: Moving from Affluence to Generosity*, 6th ed. (Nashville: W Publishing, 2015), 7–8.
10. Steven Furtick, "Blessing Is Coming," YouTube, May 5, 2020 (from September 29, 2019, sermon "Trapped in Transition," Elevation Church, Charlotte, NC), https://www.youtube.com/watch?v=rErk_Ceu-3U&ab_channel=OfficialStevenFurtick.
11. Victoria Osteen (@VictoriaOsteen), "When we live a life of giving," Twitter, September 8, 2020, 6:17 p.m.,

retweeted at PreachersNSneakers (@PRCHRSNSNKRS), "Always," Twitter, September 8, 6:19 p.m., twitter.com/PRCHRSNSNKRS/status/1303461914496962560.

Chapter 5: A Note About $1,000 Sneakers

1. PreachersNSneakers (@preachersnsneakers), "Pastor John Gray steppin out something major in the Ye'vangelical Red Octobers," Instagram, April 6, 2019, https://www.instagram.com/p/Bv6kMkWhGDa/.
2. PreachersNSneakers (@preachersnsneakers), "Pastor Troy (Gramling) likes his tees the same way he likes his Digiorno: Supreme," Instagram, July 16, 2019, https://www.instagram.com/p/Bz_SIyIh7aY/.
3. *Global Sneakers Market, by Type, by Distribution Channel, by Region, Competition, Forecast & Opportunities, 2024*, Market Report series, (n. p. Report Buyer, 2019), https://www.reportbuyer.com/product/5778896/global-sneakers-market-by-type-by-distribution-channel-by-region-competition-forecast-and-opportunities-2024.html.
4. Dennis Green, "Sneaker Makers Like Nike and Addidas Are Facing a Dilemma as Resale Is on Its Way to Becoming a $6 Billion Business," Business Insider, August 2, 2019, https://www.businessinsider.com/nike-adidas-role-sneaker-resale-market-2019-8.
5. Mayowa Aina, "They Dress from the Bottom Up: Sneakerheads Converge in D.C.," NPR, September 8, 2019, https://www.npr.org/2019/09/08/758724602/they-dress-from-the-bottom-up-sneakerheads-converge-in-d-c.
6. Tess Adamakos, "The Urban Necessities Hustle, with Jaysse Lopez," *Inked*, April 17, 2019, https://www.inkedmag.com/original-news/jaysse-lopez-from-two-js-kicks-to-urban-necesities.
7. Emmanuel Ocbazghi, "Meet the 18-Year-Old

Entrepreneur Making a Fortune Selling Rare Sneakers to Celebrities," Business Insider, January 5, 2018, https://www.businessinsider.in/meet-the-18-year-old-entrepreneur-making-a-fortune-selling-rare-sneakers-to-celebrities/articleshow/62385354.cms.

8. Ryan Cracknell, "1999 Pokemon 1st Edition Charizard Holo Sells for over $55,000," Beckett, https://www.beckett.com/news/1999-pokemon-1st-edition-charizard-holo-sells-50000/.

Chapter 6: Registered Flex Offenders

1. Ben Kirby and Jonathan Pokluda, "Jonathan 'JP' Pokluda," July 3, 2019, episode 4 of *PreachersNSneakers* podcast, MP3 audio, 27:17, https://podcasts.apple.com/us/podcast/episode-4-jonathan-jp-pokluda/id1462306991?i=1000443573621.
2. Kort Marley, *Navigating the Digital Sea: Gospel Guidance for Social Media* (Houston: Lucid Books, 2016), 35.
3. Elroy Boers et al., "Association of Screen Time and Depression in Adolescence," *JAMA Pediatrics* 173, no. 9 (July 2019): doi.org/10.1001/jamapediatrics.2019.1759.
4. Jeremy Ham, "Should Christians Pray in Public or Not?," Answers in Genesis, August 2, 2011, https://answersingenesis.org/contradictions-in-the-bible/should-christians-pray-in-public-or-not/.
5. Kimberly Jackson, "Local Church Gives Cars, Money, Homes to Members and Ministries," KTUL, December 19, 2019, https://ktul.com/news/local/church-gives-cars-money-and-homes-to-members-and-minisries.
6. Jackson, "Local Church Gives Cars."
7. VOUS Church, "Look What You Did—VOUS Gives Away $60K to Foster Care Organizations," Facebook video, November 27, 2019, https://www.facebook.com/VOUSChurch/videos/1779941642140469/.

Chapter 7: Woke Worshipers and Politicking Pastors

1. Graham Lanktree, "Trump's Independence Day Tweet Features Baptist Choir Singing MAGA Just for Him," *Newsweek*, July 4, 2017, https://www.newsweek.com/trumps-independence-day-tweet-features-maga-choir-singing-just-him-631644.
2. Jack Graham, "Why Can Evangelicals Support Trump? He's the Most Pro-Life President in U.S. History," *Dallas Morning News,* January 26, 2020, https://www.dallasnews.com/opinion/commentary/2020/01/26/jack-graham-why-can-evangelicals-support-trump-hes-the-most-pro-life-president-in-us-history/.
3. *Senate Finance Committee, Minority Staff Review of Without Walls International Church, Paula White Ministries*, prepared by Lynda F. Simmons, US Senate Committee on Finance, May 11, 2001, https://www.finance.senate.gov/imo/media/doc/WWIC%20Whites%2001-05-11.pdf.
4. Lillian Kwon, "Paula White Breaks Silence on Probes, Divorce, Benny Hinn," *Christian Post*, April 1, 2011, https://www.christianpost.com/news/paula-white-breaks-silence-on-probes-divorce-benny-hinn.html.
5. Julia Duin, "She Led Trump to Christ: The Rise of the Televangelist Who Advises the White House," *Washington Post*, November 14, 2017, https://www.washingtonpost.com/lifestyle/magazine/she-led-trump-to-christ-the-rise-of-the-televangelist-who-advises-the-white-house/2017/11/13/1dc3a830-bb1a-11e7-be94-fabb0f1e9ffb_story.html.
6. Shayne Lee and Phillip Luke Sinitiere, "Messed-Up Mississippi Girl: Paula White and the Imperfect Church," in *Holy Mavericks: Evangelical Innovators and the Spiritual Marketplace* (New York: New York University Press, 2009), 107–128.
7. Lincoln Mullen, "Just Another Sinner, Born Again,"

Atlantic, June 29, 2016, https://www.theatlantic.com/politics/archive/2016/06/trump-born-again/489269/.

8. Adele M. Stan, "Keeping Faith," Mother Jones, May/June 1996, https://www.motherjones.com/politics/1996/05/keeping-faith/.
9. Laurie Goodstein, "Obama Made Gains Among Younger Evangelical Voters, Data Show," *New York Times*, November 6, 2008, https://www.nytimes.com/2008/11/07/us/politics/07religion.html.
10. Evangelicals for Trump (website), https://evangelicals.donaldjtrump.com.
11. LifeWay Research, *Church Dropouts: Reasons Young Adults Stay or Go Between Ages 18–22* (Nashville: LifeWay Christian Resources, 2017), http://lifewayresearch.com/wp-content/uploads/2019/01/Young-Adult-Church-Dropout-Report-2017.pdf.
12. Jonathan Merritt, *A Faith of Our Own: Following Jesus Beyond the Culture Wars* (New York: FaithWords, 2012), 34.
13. Merritt, 45.
14. Peter Wehner, "The Deepening Crisis in Evangelical Christianity," *Atlantic*, July 5, 2019, https://www.theatlantic.com/ideas/archive/2019/07/evangelical-christians-face-deepening-crisis/593353/.
15. Wehner, "The Deepening Crisis."

Chapter 8: Pursue Your Promised Purpose, Particularly Proving Your Predestination

1. Laura M. Holson, "This Preacher Would Be Happy to Share Your Bowl of Açaí," *New York Times*, March 17, 2018, https://www.nytimes.com/2018/03/17/style/zoe-church-evangelical-chad-veach-pastor.html.
2. Kate Bowler, *Blessed: A History of the American Prosperity Gospel* (New York: Oxford University Press, 2013), 7.

3. Erin Duffin, "Population Distribution in the United States in 2019, by Generation," Statistica, July 20, 2020, https://www.statista.com/statistics/296974/us-population-share-by-generation/.
4. Judah Smith, quoted in Rachel Handler, "Could Going to Celebrity Church Make Me Feel Better About Trump?," MTV News, December 6, 2016, http://www.mtv.com/news/2960659/could-going-to-celebrity-church-make-me-feel-better-about-trump/.

Chapter 9: Six Flags over Jesus

1. Jack Wellman, "Why Do Churches Have Steeples? Where Did This Tradition Begin?," Patheos, September 21, 2015, https://www.patheos.com/blogs/christiancrier/2015/09/21/why-do-churches-have-steeples-where-did-this-tradition-begin/.
2. Stoyan Zaimov, "Joel Osteen's Lakewood Church Ranked America's Largest Megachurch with 52,000 Weekly Attendance," *Christian Post*, September 8, 2016, https://www.christianpost.com/news/joel-osteens-lakewood-church-ranked-americas-largest-megachurch-with-52k-in-attendance-169279.
3. Bradley Olson, "Lakewood to Buy Former Compaq Center for $7.5M," *Houston Chronicle*, March 22, 2010, https://www.chron.com/life/houston-belief/article/Lakewood-to-buy-former-Compaq-Center-for-7-5M-1715379.php.
4. "Our History," About, Gateway Church, accessed January 1, 2021, https://gatewaypeople.com/about/history.
5. "The Prestonwood Story," Our Story, Prestonwood Baptist Church, accessed January 1, 2021, http://www.prestonwood.org/about/our-story.
6. Dan Daley, "Fellowship Church: Embracing

Contemporary Worship Styles," April 26, 2020, https://www.soundandcommunications.com/fellowship-church-embracing-contemporary-worship-styles/.

7. James K. Wellman Jr., Katie E. Corcoran, and Kate J. Stockly, *High on God: How Megachurches Won the Heart of America* (New York: Oxford University Press, 2020), 2.
8. Instagram poll, Nature's Table Café at Northland Church (@NaturesTableNorthland), Facebook page, https://www.facebook.com/NaturesTableNorthland/.
9. Instagram poll, see 2019 campus map of Willow Creek Community Church, Barrington, Illinois, https://www.willowcreek.org/-/media/images/1-0-locations/1-1-south-barrington/sbcampusmap2019.pdf.
10. Instagram poll, see "The Tanks," Inspiring Body of Christ Church, https://www.ibocchurch.org/the-tanks.
11. Kate Bowler, *Blessed: A History of the American Prosperity Gospel* (New York: Oxford University Press, 2013), 102–3.
12. Brittany De Lea, "Best Cities for People with Student Loan Debt," Fox Business, May 7, 2019, https://www.foxbusiness.com/economy/best-cities-student-loan-debt.
13. "Little Drummer Boy—Prestonwood GOC 2019," YouTube video posted by John Muzyka, December 15, 2019 (Gift of Christmas performance at Prestonwood Baptist Church, Plano, Texas), https://www.youtube.com/watch?v=XGlKWBkFfBQ.
14. "The Prestonwood Story."
15. "About Prestonwood Pregnancy Center," About Us, Prestonwood Pregnancy Center, https://prestonwoodpregnancy.org/about-us/.
16. Nicholas Sakelaris, "Southlake-Based Gateway Church Confirms It Will Cut Staff by 10–15 Percent," *Fort Worth Star-Telegram,* updated April 21, 2017, https://

www.star-telegram.com/news/local/community
/northeast-tarrant/article145759799.html.

17. Cameron Strang et al., "Episode 792: Judah Smith," *RELEVANT Podcast*, March 24, 2020, MP3 audio, 43:09, https://www.relevantmagazine.com/podcast /episode-792-judah-smith.
18. John Pavlovitz, "Remember, the Bible Never Mentions a Building Called 'Church,'" *Relevant*, June 24, 2019, https://relevantmagazine.com/god/remember-bible-never -mentions-building-called-church/.
19. Pavlovitz, "Remember."
20. Timothy A. Songster, *Healthy Church by Design: The Synergy Between Buildings and Church Health* (Spring Hill, TN: Rainer Publishing, 2018), 47.
21. "In the Halls of the Vatican," *Coffilosophy* (blog), July 16, 2012, https://coffilosophy.com/2012/07/16/in -the-halls-of-the-vatican/.

Chapter 10: Church Merch

1. "VOUS," Church Shop, Wayback Machine, April 26, 2020, https://web.archive.org/web/20200426222538; https://merch.vouschurch.com/.
2. "Vous Church Easter Sunday Quarantine 2020 T-Shirt," Teelotus.com, accessed January 1, 2021, https://teelotus .com/product/
vous-church-easter-sunday-quarantine-2020/.
3. Will Kenton, "Brand," Investopedia, March 27, 2020, https://www.investopedia.com/terms/b/brand.asp.
4. Sam Schube, "Hypepriests: The Grail-Wearing Pastors Who Dress Like Justin Bieber," *GQ*, August 7, 2017, https://www.gq.com/story/hypepriests-pastors-who-dress -like-justin-bieber.
5. Schube, "Hypepriests."
6. Whitney Bauck, "Is Church Merch the Next Big Thing

in Streetwear?," Fashionista, October 16, 2018, https://fashionista.com/2017/08/church-merch-clothing-streetwear-trend.
7. Bauck, "Church Merch."

Chapter 11: Callout Culture, Christian Twitter, and Clowning Pastors

1. Allen R. Myerson, "Southern Baptist Convention Calls for Boycott of Disney," *New York Times*, June 19, 1997, https://www.nytimes.com/1997/06/19/us/southern-baptist-convention-calls-for-boycott-of-disney.html.
2. Jonathan Merritt, "Evangelicals Perfected Cancel Culture. Now It's Coming for Them," Religion News Service, June 17, 2020, https://religionnews.com/2020/06/17/evangelicals-perfected-cancel-culture-now-its-coming-for-them/.
3. John Piper (@JohnPiper), "Farewell Rob Bell," Twitter, February 26, 2011, 3:09 p.m., https://twitter.com/JohnPiper/status/41590656421863424?s=20.
4. Jon Meacham, "TIME 100: Rob Bell," *TIME*, April 21, 2011, http://content.time.com/time/specials/packages/article/0,28804,2066367_2066369_2066460,00.html.
5. Jonathan Merritt, "Lauren Daigle and the Lost Art of Discernment," *Atlantic*, December 8, 2018, https://www.theatlantic.com/ideas/archive/2018/12/let-lauren-daigle-be-unsure-about-lgbt-relationships/577651/.
6. Kate Shellnutt, "Christians in the Age of Callout Culture," *Christianity Today*, December 16, 2019, https://www.christianitytoday.com/ct/2020/january-february/christians-in-age-of-callout-culture.html.
7. Shellnutt, "Christians in the Age of Callout Culture."
8. "What Does the Bible Say About Gossip?," Got Questions, last updated January 2, 2020, https://www.gotquestions.org/gossip-Bible.html.

9. "What Does the Bible Say?"
10. "What Does the Bible Say?"
11. Leonardo Blair, "Pastor Kirbyjon Caldwell, Adviser to Obama and Bush, Pleads Guilty to Fraud," *Christian Post*, March 12, 2020, https://www.christianpost.com/news/pastor-kirbyjon-caldwell-adviser-to-obama-and-bush-pleads-guilty-to-fraud.html.
12. Shellnutt, "Christians in the Age of Callout Culture."

Chapter 12: Wow! You Read Till the End

1. Stephen R. Graves, *Flourishing: Why Some People Thrive While Others Just Survive* (Fayetteville, AR: KJK Publishing, 2015), 31.
2. Ronald J. Sider, *Rich Christians in an Age of Hunger: Moving from Affluence to Generosity*, 6th ed. (Nashville: W Publishing, 2015), 190–91.
3. John Cortines and Gregory Baumer, *God and Money: How We Discovered True Riches at Harvard Business School* (Carson, CA: Rose Publishing, 2016), 45.
4. Jonathan "JP" Pokluda, *Welcoming the Future Church: How to Reach, Teach, and Engage Young Adults* (Grand Rapids: Baker Books, 2020), 81–83.
5. Paul Tripp, "Should Christians Be on Social Media?," *Ask Paul Tripp* (podcast), January 18, 2020, https://www.paultripp.com/ask-paul-tripp/posts/should-christians-be-on-social-media.
6. Cortines and Baumer, *God and Money*, 26.

ABOUT THE AUTHOR

Ben Kirby is the creator of the viral social media sensation PreachersNSneakers, where he caused an uproar after showing the values of what clothing preachers were wearing on stage across the globe. Along with growing from zero to hundreds of thousands of followers in just a few weeks, his work has been featured in the *New York Times*, *The New Yorker*, *The Wallstreet Journal*, Buzzfeed, Fox News, Complex, and many more. He also hosts the popular podcast with the ultra-creative name *The PreachersNSneakers Podcast*.

His background is unconventional for this type of movement. He served as a Marine Corps logistics officer, serving tours in Eastern Europe across Romania, Kosovo, Bosnia, Italy, and Spain, leading hundreds of Marines and Sailors to protect the United States and its allies. After his time in the Marines, Ben served as vice president of operations for a tech-enabled services firm, where he not only served in a leadership role but also helped manage a multimillion dollar operation. He holds his BSBA in marketing management from the University of Arkansas and his MBA in strategy and entrepreneurship from the

Cox School of Business at Southern Methodist University. He now works full-time as a business owner, podcaster, and author in Texas, where he lives with his wife, Stacy (with a baby on the way), and two Labrador retrievers, Gumbeaux and Roux.

When not making Christians feel uncomfortable, Ben spends his time fly-fishing, playing drums, flipping sneakers, writing comedy, eating all the foods, smoking exquisite meats, trying different libations (responsibly), and looking for new entrepreneurial endeavors.